Can't Beat Them, Join Them @ The boardroom.

Living American dream

Pelly Kraft

ISBN: 0692476563
ISBN 13: 9780692476567
Library of Congress Control Number: 2015910404
pamela Moses, Mesa, AZ

Preface

THE CLOCK IS ticking, nothing seems to interest you anymore, the odd and discouraging news flash on your TV screen is always the same. Families in distress, the stock market is down, what's next ? You ask yourself? Well you can put your best foot forward and try something new. Out of your comfort zone you've got to try, change is sweet anything is possible with just a minimum interest Where game changers are involved, there's no need waiting to be inspired someday. Follow the trend, they are self-motivated. Courage a midst tough times and succeed where others have failed, you can too.

To friends, you are great!
Thank you !
Pelly Kraft.

Introduction

THIS IS FORSTER! Answering a phone call ! Then.. Silence ! Ha ha ha! That hearty laugh filled the upper deck office ! That was more like Forster, he was listening to a phone conversation, she is French! He exclaimed! Honey, I didn't understand a word you said! And you are looking for Pete?, That's right! She answered. He is my business partner, not what you think but thanks for the best wishes, Pete was married to some dainty Australian lady. I bet they do not eat hamburgers over there! So, I will get Pete' on the line, please hold! Walking down the stairs, he was still smiling about the unfortunate information people get to assume, hey Pete', come up here, he calls Pete who was engrossed in some conversation with a regular customer who loved the coffee brewed at that part of the morning! Hey! The lady wants to get a clear direction to the coffee shop, she is visiting from France, someone told her about our small coffee shop! Amazing! Pete drags his left foot which became tingly from sitting down for a while working on the taxes.. Apparently Charlie's horse does not spare anyone.. He gave the customer a wicked smile, still wincing in pain! Old age! Forster blasted from across the staircase... Come up here please, she waiting!

So you can imagine what Forster and Pete went through, they did not just dream but treaded upon it! The investments later brought a huge success to them.

1
The Boardroom.

ANDRE'S NAME WAS about success, he had great Ideas to share all the time but how could he make it work in such a business set up? He needed a team of managers to work miracles using talent Some math and expertise!

On a serious note, he had to create the infamous board to handle and to help him tackle certain urgent matters. His plan? Better governance, better marketing skills, keep ahead in sales, he thought for several weeks before making a final decision.

The first boardroom I attended gave me a different insight and changed my thinking about retail or any other business In place.

06:15 PM... It seemed like forever, waiting for the meeting to start. I saw most sales managers logging in, one by one, their gadgets lighting up the room which was partly lit. It was a little different from the old school conferences or any board meeting. Of course, this was different! I need all the resources I can get to pull this through! Andre' would say...

The finance department had more meetings than all for systems updates for new plastic tenders and how to adjust to the current digital world. This included, handling money transfers outside financial institutions, what measures to take, correct forms to fill and the limit on keeping public records as required by the governing laws.

Service clerks are expected just to do their jobs by following correct procedures, this however is after proper training and a supervisor walking them through the process. It is that Important to give the right training if you want them to do their job correctly.

Today's meeting started with classical music, on the background, it was like no other meetings I have attended before and definitely a serious business.

After the opening speech by the main chair, each and every man-ager in attendance gave reports of what the daily needs were, daily sales and trends.

That included how to identify star merchandise in each depart-ment, necessary changes, why and what creates delays on delivery and how to handle the situation without wasting too much time and of cause any other business that needed discussion.

Department managers are expected to monitor very closely

If their departments made any progress and also be in charge of smooth running of the departments which included working closely with sales representatives who are in constant contact with guests to the store, proper communication and mentoring to these employees was very necessary to give that perfect picture every retailer want to achieve great customers service.

so all these managers were in charge of their project areas and if there was need for changes, that was the time to do it because what makes sense is to have that correct merchandise on the shelf when needed and in good condition, if you get what I mean, Andre said.

Yes, we do understand that part well, the group answered back!

That means proper handling of the product and correct shelving or display for that matter. If your department ends up with too much overstock, then you need to change that by training your stocking team but not before proper labels that explains merchandise on the box is placed on it for easy access and re- stocking the temporary warehouse within the premises.

It also takes a smart sales representative to help create a great outlook and better presentation.

Of course well zoned shelf, spread out and pretty look with price labels and no identifiable gaps because this freaks out your guests... What I mean by that is, they wonder if the company is going out of business that's a picture you don't wanna paint! He said.

For our 24 hour airport Businesses, we have to step up re-stocking to meet the traffic and availability of the merchandise.

One time guest on transit will only remember what met the eye at that time or what they did not find in stock especially if the company advertisement implies that the company carries it, however stagnant merchandise holding company's money, can be discontinued, placed at a reduced price, sell it and get the original purchase price, stay afloat, create a room for a moving merchandise and ready for a new theme.

Remember, surveys are important too... They are our guidance to show us what our guests prefer and the need to carry certain merchandise...

That doesn't mean we can't stock certain merchandise that creates impulse sales... He smiled in the middle of that sentence In Most cases, you want these guests in your store, even better if we can satisfy our guest's needs..

The trick, bring our guests to our doors, and then, they can see what else we've got and try to keep them under one roof... By that I mean one stop shop and they are out... Saves time, right? He asked.

The Boardroom consists of branch manager, the assisting managers, department managers and all in management status.

Ideas and recommendations helped guide the board as to which way forward as you already know what previous discussions that all supervisors have the capability to solve simple problems about sales but mind boggling issues are to be brought to the boardroom for discussions so we can find quick solutions to urgent matters.

It's all about sales, making profits and staying on top of the game, don't you agree?

It is pretty much what any successful business owner would do to succeed which includes good management and staying focused!

Of course!

Everyone seems to understand it all!

Andre was determined to prove that success came through hard work not wishes!

He was put to test by Forster and Pete to do a better job.

Forster and Pete, two friends different backgrounds with the same vision, big Ideas and to most, inspiration and the will to do it!

The coffee shop business was getting slow over the past season, and making ends meet was becoming a problem.

Many months past, they had to think of what's next, Pete was not ready to go back to France and perfect his Art but how about something totally different?

After consulting with friends and some business consultants, they settled on trying retail business in a different way. Pete was in agony, his first thought was to travel around the globe and get new ideas on how they could succeed along those lines when they could get to convince one of their friends to sell his warehouse not far from the boardwalk, they could start by getting some stock of any kind and deliver it where their clients wanted it, they just needed to figure out how to do it!

Forster had a lot of experience on the dock, logistics was his thing!

He blames his thinning hair to it! It was still a challenge to both of them trying something new.

For two months they went digging on any information they could get, Pete' went to Paris to attend a grand exhibition in Vermont, how could he miss it? Art runs through his blood...

That break was needed, he thought!

As he called Forster to explain his experience after not flying for years, Forster was also at a concert, classical

Music calmed his nerves!

He later returned Pete's call and told him, you'd better come back with fresh ideas! His laugh across the alley was recognizable!

Hey! 'Bonne nuit'... See you when you get back, he told Pete!

Later that year, they were set to try out their plans. After they hired Andre, they had no Idea, they might have just started a journey that would change things, high end customer service and more!

Respect and value are key factors...

How could you say you failed without ever trying to succeed?

The only way to overcome it is to take that one step! Pete consoled himself... In his artistic version, He was thinking a loud while Forster was working on a master plan, charts hanging loosely on one corner of the veneer walls, files scattered on top of his desk, we might just realize our dreams! He said.

When they finally made their decision, Andre was the right man for the job!

Andre qualifying best amongst two hundred applicants, his resume stood out and he was best pick ever!

As things went on they thought Andre had great Ideas which they decided to adapt to those skills and used them where applicable in all the stores they owned.

This was the way it will be, take it or leave it!

It's a dream come true... Pete would comment to his friends all the time. Andre obviously brought success to these two friends

For several years, they thought the coffee shop was it!

Never did it cross their minds that it would be a flop!

When they started off, it was just a small coffee house, a reason to get out of the house after retiring from active work... So they built an upper deck to store coffee beans and a small office for Forster since he preferred some quite time while working on his accounts books.

During peak hours Jeanette, Pete's wife would help out but had to leave to pick up the kids from school.

Pete and Forster struck a great relationship since the time they met at an auction in Louisville, the musical instruments they were trying to find made them strike a conversation.

Pete's French accent brought curiosity as to why he would ever think about business in that part of neighborhood, people would ask but his dreams did not die simply because of negative comments, he was geared to steer on. After they were done with their selection on the type of employees they wanted, there was no stopping in the middle, skilled personnel required little training, they could reach for the stars!

Al', Bob and Josh joined Andre, the set up was from the scratch, several years past with a lot of success came their way, it was time to spread their wings to other areas, a little upgrade and transition to a smaller complex easily accessible, easy to manage type.

Forster thought it would give them that opportunity to stay connected and close to their guests. Needless to say, those that shopped at any of their branches felt like part of the business, to me they were part of it!

They remained loyal for years and that brought about success that they are currently proud of!

Forster played a part in this, he took time to talk to each guest that came his way and probably shared a joke!

I mean he was a free spirit kind of guy.

From the upgrade they recently did, the profit margin realized over a period of time gave them the confidence to carry on and to believe the future was bright

2
Clues to success.

AFTER FORSTER AND Pete started the coffee shop in upstate New York, they were doing well.

They hired Jasper, A flamboyant witty kind of person..

He was hands on, people's favorite but was cautious to maintain business-like kind of look most of the times.

Forster was okay with that, it met his Concerns about keeping standards.

They had their ups and downs but they did not give up even at the worse tax season, most businesses on a nose dive, the stock market affecting more people, Pete hated the idea of losing so much on his stocks, it hurts!

He would shake his head explaining it!

Even though things were tough in the initial stages, they Stuck with their original plans and finally saw some doors open for them.

After dealing some blows, they were skeptical but envisioned the finish line and that means achieving their goals. They almost ignored digital networking being old school but it certainly did help get their names out there..

Forster does not believe in half-truths, very doubtful at first of certain ads, he'd rather do things the old fashion way but the present life seems to have a higher demand and it's hard to cope in the business world if you are not competitive, Pete always reminds him, that they've got to do better act better even just try to perform their daily business better than their competitor!

They remained open to new things and reminded themselves that at this time and age it's all a about compatibility and compliance!

At the present time, Pete was more concerned about all the avenues that would bring about tools to unlock potentials to a successful growth, way to go! I thought! Jasper had skills from retail set up before being hired By Forster and Pete so, he was an asset to work with. His Slogan, be ready! He went on to explain to cashiers working for the company how to manage time while serving guests to remember to be efficient and make it your style of doing things, he quotes!

Loretta, a former computer whiz was good with numbers I can't forget when she joined the Company perusing through that web as if it was child's play when she finds it, meaning the Missing figures, she would go, boom! Got it!

How easy was it for her I would ask

I found out that she had to skip a class to move to a higher grade because she was extra bright She was always ahead of the teacher by doing her own research, won the geek of the year during her year book!

She won most competitions that most geeks wishes they were invited to! Reason? They had all the confidence that anything digital was their cup of tea, in this case coffee!

And now it was her part to bring it home the way the company wants it!

As far as I know most companies read or give you a document that states the company policies and no doubt they will be monitoring closely anything that involves finances!

she was certainly good at what she did, she was this happy girl, sort of 'don't worry about it' type of person, heavy set but pretty always bubbly, it was hard to get mad at her when she made a mistake, she would genuinely be apologetic and follow it up with a bewitching smile!

The frequent compliment she got, was more about her beautiful teeth and not for her brains which deserved more recognition!

And by the way she had some pearly White teeth!

No coffee stains? I thought... But then there are wearable stain removers being bright she may have thought about that too, good for her!

No doubt, the team was great and in the process Introduced programs that were customer friendly, needless to say, the business thrived for the better. When Andre joined the company, Jasper's job was to manage the coffee houses mainly at the local Airports which later spread across the country and later same year went global, a taste of good Coffee, Arabica or Colombian, brewed to satisfy your taste!

what couldn't be better? They love it out there!

He would say... Good for you man!

His friends encouraged him. On the other hand Andre had his style too...

He says, grilling anew employee too much is not necessary give them right tools to do the job, you should know that employee who has what it takes to do the job when you see them, their personality speaks volumes and their willingness to do their job.

Years of good work, the owners were proud of Andre.

He was certainly the right man for the job, they paid him well. Staying with the winners, Andre was the one to stick with, high ratings, the best was yet to come, they were happy.

Pete and Forster rarely attended the Boardroom but when they did, their main concern was to make sure that the company's strongest asset which was good management was maintained.

Forster told the managers that if the company has everything except proper management, it may prosper but eventually will fall and since we have come a long way with this business, it is the last thing we want so we want to stay on the right track to make the grades because profits will display itself, he said!

This boardroom we must focus on management techniques, why do I say this? It's because this has evolved from what successful people have learned by struggling with their mistakes. We must avoid mistakes by keeping a close eye on the recurring problems and find a better way to deal with it.

Every kinds of businesses, large or small make errors, however large corporations can absorb costly mistakes that might otherwise prove fatal for the small or medium sized enterprise. The margin for error in a small business is slim because it is easily identifiable but creating loses knowingly is unacceptable.

The pitfalls Include :-

1. Failure to plan,
2. paying attention
3. marketing errors
4. Insufficient Leadership.
5. To expound on that, failure to plan can be the most devastating business mistake.

Lack of planning weakens the entire efforts of the company, you don't want to be part of failure but be part of success. Pacing the floor, Forster looked directly at the people he thought should take his advice seriously and told them to take note.

When you plan ahead of time, you take advantage Of opportunities, establish and realize goals and objectives of the company. You will also be able to monitor your progress and meeting them.

There are a few things that we have to put within our plans in terms of merchandise and promotion.

The company budget will serve as a basis for the measurement and control of progress towards planned objectives, Pete added the last word in case Forster forgot to mention it!

3
Brand Selection.

THE LAST BOARDROOM left us thinking, but as the notion we have every day that American family will always have something to snack on, does not mean we stock just whatever appeals to the eye but focus on better brands. Well as you know we have a digital program that separates each brand and recommends the best poll to the system which we later assess and work with it as the guest's best choice.

To finally settle on what brands to promote and sell, Serious selection was conducted by qualified personnel measures on quality brands, better packaging and durability. Their recommendations was valuable to the company to keep the standards high.

Loretta's job was to monitor these sales, she was used to the up and down figures but Certainly that survey, or whatever you want to call it, I told Al, is a great guide when it comes to selecting correct brands for long term stocks.

We had to take a tour around the Store to see a few things that had been changed, as we passed through the back alley, Al' pointed out what needs to be done after a wind storm destroyed Part of the roof outside. This needs to be done as soon as possible, I agreed with him.

I prepared to call the right technician for the job, I know that this store is fairly clean and so nothing ugly should be seen from outside.

I made my way in after giving instructions to the technician on what needs to be done. I caught a glimpse of Bob having a hard time with his computer through the crack at the door which was halfway closed, he just needed to work fast, no back logs allowed.

Main season switch was approaching and he had to work around the clock to accomplish this knowing that Andre did not accept "No" for an answer, you have to find Plan 'B' if 'A' did not work, to him, there was no dead end, there's always a way out!

That actually proves why the ratings were up, with good sales blowing the roof, it was something to be proud of!

He made sure he reminded everybody of his latest achievements, which was about moving above the expected million dollars Margin mark per quarter. To me, I thought it was great but that includes participation of every employee who played a role in it.

Of course Bob said with his eyes wide open to signify, I should not make a comment at that time… I know that hard work pays, okay!

To cut the story short, I asked if he still needed my help to which he declined and so I made my exit.

4
Second Deck.

TROY HAD JUST joined the company, he was happy to finally have someone he could rely on, season was changing from winter to spring, soon it would be extremely busy at the registers.

Bob walked him through the store and at one Point, he pointed at part of the second deck mentioning where spare parts for motor vehicles were kept which included bay area and all the accessories in stock.

Walking around with Bob and the vendors, was part of knowing and keeping good inventory of the products the company had in stock so if a guest needed some help on how to locate the items, it would not be hard identifying them if the Items were within the store. For those merchandise at the top, use a ladder for God's sake otherwise you will tumble and fall with bolts spilling all over the place, hard to trace all of them, let's just say it can be a great disaster to both employees and guests!

I could see Troy's wide grin, probably drawing the scene in his mind!

One of the vendors told Bob not to worry, that he was intelligent enough...

I know, Bob said, but it's my duty to repeat it to every new employee in case it slipped their mind, they would remember this walk, Agreed! Troy replied

Troy, was just that articulate supervisor who prioritizes on Solving guest's problems. The counseling job at a local School helped him to stay calm even at a tough situation most retailers face with their guests. You would find unsatisfied ones, the problem creed group, the tough to handle group, the grouchy ones, the smiley ones, the loner, the 'I do not I appreciate you talking to me!'

The list goes on and on to the 'I don't need anybody' type, check me out as soon as you can' type…. You'd see expressions on their faces which reminds the attending clerk to stay out of their damn business. Best thing to do? keep the greeting official and short. In most cases, you'd see the mood change if the clerk was fast and efficient!

Always keep your smile soft but remain official as much as you can, Troy would mention this to any new employment Most of them want to hit the check out and get out of there in a flash, you've got to know how to handle them all! And why would someone not want to be greeted?

I asked? You can never really tell why it happens but there are all sorts of things that can bring stress to people in general, could be pressure from office, a second job or just tired and would be pleased to get home with their groceries as quick as they can, but I know you are bright enough to know who you are dealing with and knows the trend.

Of course! The clerk replied! Just follow your daily routines as you attend to such guests!

Troy asked the clerks who were willing to lend an ear standing next to his desk. Oh yes! They assured him.

Mmm I wondered, I mean they were late before they got to the store… But how could I know where they were rushing to? May be pick up a kid at school or attend to a sick relative, who knows! Troy laughed at my comment…

He said, if the first guest shows signs of 'do not disturb' and does not want to be greeted, keep going with the checkout process and complete the transaction, no doubt the next guest behind will definitely take it!

Amazing?

Oh yeah, over a period of time, you get to master all these things! He said

I was kind of glad I didn't have to deal with that kind of stuff daily but rarely. I could do well with just studying merchandise, stock it, sell it, make money and increase volume.

Josh had been busy the whole week, many guests visiting the store almost at the same time, anyway this was expected every time the season changes when people are either Updating or involved in an outdoor activity, Josh was a nice guy but he had a little bit of a straying eye but this time, it was Pete's wife that needed his help whom he had no Idea was the CEO's wife!

Forster was walking to the main front podium when he got a glimpse of Josh leaning too close while talking to Jeanette!

Being a bright middle aged guy, he cleared his throat to let Josh know he noticed his move and cautioned him to keep off Josh definitely needed some words of wisdom, you want to keep your job? Stay out of Pete's Interest!

Josh was grateful, he said he did not know who she was and apologized!

What does that tell you? Forster asked him treat everyone with respect, he replied. Good boy! Let's keep it that way, Forster told him and left!

Josh was a little shaken after realizing what just happened!

He tried to catch up with Forster still thinking how he was going to say it...

Forster looking back at him surprised! What's your Problem?

He asked Josh...

Sir, you are not going to tell Pete? Are you kidding me? When did you think I could be involved in some gossip?

I'm sorry sir... Well get back to work, I will not tell him and kept walking to his car. Jeanette was French, her parents moved from France to Australia where they were both teachers and ended up settling there.

Jeanette was born in Melbourne, Australia. You couldn't miss a fine wine at her dinner table, I just wondered what her wine Cellar looked like? That day she had her friends from a book club joining her for lunch that afternoon so she needed good wine real fast which she couldn't find at the shelf but somehow she hoped Josh could help her find that particular selection.

she had striking look, who couldn't notice Her? Josh said later to his friends after realizing who she was. She was fair and tall, hazel eyes, she kept her hair neatly to a shoulders length.

Forster on the other hand, knows how hard it was for Pete to date but when he did, it was Jeanette!

He recalls when him and Pete were out up in the glaciers a few years ago, she was a real good skier no doubt about it! This way, she pointed them to the right direction, as they were lost due to flaky winds and could not see the trail. When they reached the bottom of the peaks, she took off her mask and Pete's jaws Dropped!

Forster gave him a minute to think, then tapped him lightly on his shoulders, hey! You can at least ask her for her number... Don't just stare! Forster told him... Jeanette was smiling... Pete took two steps towards her and thanked her for the help. He introduced himself, Forster and was brave enough to ask her for her telephone number, she hesitated but gave him her number anyway...

After a short chat, she skid down the slopes, Pete watched her as she disappeared between the pines!

That was the beginning of a long term relationship.

The wedding came a year later at a secluded private country club attended by a handful of friends and relatives.

The French Riviera was their next Destination!

Forster threw them a lavish party when they returned to New York!

As for Forster, he was taking a break from serious dating since his opera singing girlfriend was swept off her feet by some kind of prince charming!

I could have married her... You know! With that expression, anyone could tell how Forster felt about her!

He told Pete' that afternoon he was returning the ring to the jeweler, he had not completely forgotten about her, he was heartbroken...

One evening before they broke up, he went out of his way and prepared for her, a romantic dinner at his mansion, she never showed up!

After frantic phone calls, thinking she was having difficulty getting to his place, he found out she was never coming... On the other end of the phone call to his surprise, he heard I'm sorry Forster! He was stunned! You mean you are not coming? He asked her. The answer was in the affirmative!

Makes you wonder what happened, just when you think things are going great, then all these? He was lost for weeks...

Pete had to go and find him and bring him to the Coffee shop!

This was like a big punch to his gut! He was going to ask her to marry him that evening he had to return the rock to the jewelry store. He was very open and bold, as he went into the store he told his friend, Bill the owner of the jewelry store where diamonds speak the language of the rich and famous!

she said No, man...

Ooh, that's too bad!

I thought she was in love with you Forster? Bill asked.

Exchanging some awkward laughs... Forster told him just to put the money back to the card! Bill, beckoning to a clerk standing by the display to take the ring and start reimbursement process to Forster.

Certainly sir! The Clerk told him, Sorry about that sir! Thank you! I will be fine, I'm just glad I didn't propose to the wrong person, it would have been a disaster!

The clerk, looking at the ticket Swearing in his mind, why would someone buy such a huge rock if he wasn't even sure this girl would say yes to him? But instead he thought of something else, a smile, have a good day sir! He told Forster.

Thanks, you too! Forster replied back as he was walking towards the door and to his car.

While, it was Forster's pain, Sue, one of the clerks at the store, was giggling, Probably thinking a loud, mumbling words, she said if someone like Forster proposed,

Oh! He can put that big old rock on my finger at any time! Laughing but trying to hide it...

I would be like Yes! Yes! Imitating some unseen figure in her head!

People just don't spend a lot of money on a rock like this one if they didn't love the girl, too bad!

Anyway he's a cool guy with money, he will find the right girl soon! Sue?

The clerk over heard her, what do you mean? He asked her.

Can't you see that the man is heartbroken?

Jeez! Have some sympathy!

Just commenting! Sue replied, pretending to sympathize with Forster.

Any way bad things happen to good people, she said that in a consoling kind of mood!

But just like most jewelers who sell certain types Of rings, this was not a surprise! A few times that happens, as much as they expect the customer to keep the ring, it's usually the opposite, this goes with taste, size and who knows what the partner likes!

The clerk said he had seen that a lot especially in the past two years, people just don't seem to make up their minds in time for their own wedding or the economy is taking control on major decisions! The story you get is either, the girl didn't like the style or she changed her mind, the story line is long. Some prefer solitaire while others like princess cut or just anything big in the famous triangular shape and must be neatly cut from a precious stone, even better if it's the famous emerald uniquely designed shape, it definitely stands out! Some consider the gesture to be priceless! You could never tell what will happen, the clerk said, you keep your fingers crossed and hope they don't return a fake diamond!

The only good thing was that most customers stayed true because the special order registry kept records of their names and also on the final transaction document, their risk of going to jail would be great if they did something stupid!

But as far as rejections, those are expected, it does not matter how big or small the rock is, the commitment part, is what brings everything to a screeching halt!

If these clerks can tell you what they see or hear every day on both bad and happy endings, the reasons are enormous, but they don't kiss and tell!

Act of professionalism was required of them and the need to keep details of their customers private, Bill made sure they understood that part well, he didn't want to lose his good name to a desperate clerk and besides, he paid them well.

5
Time & Season.

BOB HAD BEEN working on tough issues this week, I knew he had something up his sleeve, he could hardly be seen on sales floor. I guess he was concerned about factors that could reduce chances of having accidents within the Premises.

Isles have to be consumer friendly, properly placed pegs, flyers and updated displays. Safety comes first so everyone here has to participate and abide by the company rules. Card board displays must be hooked to a well fixed or stationery frame, he mentions that all the time, I get it being sued is equally expensive! His goal always is to find better ways to beat competitor and not going against them sometimes, it's a war you can't win, so by playing your cards right makes it easy to win! If we sell quality merchandise right price in the right season, keep constant supplies and proper marketing strategies, better packaging, pausing in the middle, I could almost see a smile at the corner of his mouth while he said this!

You can't go wrong and by the way winners don't think about losing they just do it!

Minding my own business, walking past Bob's Office on the hall way there were vending machines which were filled with natural foods, I was hungry so I couldn't help but look to that direction, I didn't care much about what was inside the machine but was just thinking of how I could fill my hungry tummy. I wasn't certain if the vending machine could provide what I needed for lunch but I knew I had to make a choice!

I guess this was the healthy choice of foods packed to go, thanks to Brenda, a former Yoga Instructor turned head of department of organic foods and natural products.

Bob had just dashed back to the office carrying what he had just bought and placed it on top of his work table... As for me, after scanning through what was inside the vending machines, I thought for a moment... Not me, today I'm a little hungry, I break the rules Sometimes, that good old juicy hamburger seems to be the best choice! Sorry Brenda!

Coming back from my quick lunch out, I was feeling like I could tackle anything, definitely feeling happy about my meal.

Bob was still at his desk, he had his files on his bosom, he was probably done with his work. Finishing his snack, he held a few price tags for a new product added to the design Galore, he was worried about stagnant seasonal products and wondered if we missed the season.

He stood up and asked me to join him as we walked through to the galore, he saw that some employees did not complete the assignment he had asked them to do and was not pleased, he intended to find out why?

He said he did not mind critics but employees with wrong attitude? That type of employee does not have place in this type of business!

He was definitely disturbed by this!

He expected a good reflection to our guests, he paused for a moment as if he was thinking of something major to say, when he finally said it with some passion... In times of stiff competition, guests rule, they are the reason we open these doors pointing to the main entrance!

After all the training and the mentoring, I expect excellence in both ways, no stepping on your employees toes Remember we must try and keep those good employees who have what it takes, those you can depend on to do the right thing even when you are not supervising, those are the ones I consider an asset to the company, everyone matters here and no excuses!

Bob is the guy you want to ask questions on how to go about tasks, because he pretty much had an answer ready for you, if you asked about job related issues, making my job a little easier, I thought. He told me the company had to look far and wide for a different brand selection, taking in consideration the sale price, meaning if necessary, look for more free markets that want to work with our rates.

We had to think of those big sales deals we can make, for example institutions like filming and training schools as well as recording studios they both expect us to stock all digital C3 balance components, packages in place to update with the digital age, it's all about meeting our guests needs, right? Must I say this to you, all the time?

No! I said, being sarcastic, I told him I remembered the tone he said it and when... And that my memory card wasn't full yet!

Remember institutions would rather buy from us than direct from the manufacturer itself, he smiled and explained to me in the most simplest Way.

Okay, here is why, shipping and handling for fewer products cost more to one time buyer and price is not negotiable!

Now luckily for us, thanks to Forster who established the networking channel and trend while still at the dock business. As we speak it's as quick as making a call and talk to the right person, seal the deal and have it shipped. Two way agreement, done deal without doubts!

We have an upper hand, we pick our price if the deal is good, meaning we can lower our prices and make quick sales.

This enables the company to make profits and is the main goal.

The next step is to proceed with documentations and have these type of merchandise delivered to our shipment docks and to our cargo facilities, shorten delivery time and less change of hands and finally make your customer happy.

The best plan? Continue to stay ahead of your game and keep the business running!

Now you understand why?

Aah... Yes! Any good information is worth listening to, that's for sure, I told him.

He was exactly right.

6
Digital Applications.

UPDATING TO THE new technology took quite a while but it was inevitable this change was coming, there is no other way it could be better especially if we are to stay in touch with the rest of the world in terms of business.

Without being compliant digitally, operations can be difficult especially accessing certain data image needed for work. Systems work better with un-interrupted communications, Josh said,

He is Mr. gadget man..

He said things were swift if only people in his network knew how to communicate better...

All in all as you both have experienced, it's so much about meeting goals, my team here including Kristy, a fellow supervisor has not let me down, at least I can say the whole team has been able to cope with busy times at hand and I have not seen negative attitude, so I can say they have met their goals for this year.

Josh and Kristy have been friends since she climbed the ladder josh hoped for something more than just boyfriend and girlfriend thing but work ethics made this thought, access denied issue!

So he had to either go to the coffee Shop or change departments which he hated because he wanted to stay just where he was!

Kristy was sharp, she got to operate the codes on the first day she got the job which makes her, a gadget whiz!

Touch screen access as she says, that's a job simplified! Transactions done quick and less stressful.

Kristy was a party girl, she could not stand boring boyfriends, she wanted to be where action is after Work, that was just her, some people never change irrespective of their job or title job face, was slightly different than the party face!

Josh, on the other hand was a gentleman and would have preferred to take his time before he could make any decisions. They went out a few times, and to most of the other employees, it was an open secret that they were sharing more than a French kiss!

Josh had figured out a better way to break off the relationship before Forster found out, he would be disappointed, he recalls, it was one of those things that just happen, you can't help it!

He told his friends, last time he watched football with them at the local wine bar. His buddies, told him just like it is! Man you tripped and you need to pull your head from a' slang', I can't even mention here...

Friends are helpful because they see the need to keep you on the right track, you may or may not like it but it's the absolute truth!

He finally got it!

Josh started his new trick by giving lame excuses to Kristy, no frothy drinks after work and he stopped going to the Bowling alley with her again because that was one of Pete's stops before going home on a Saturday afternoon as he later found out the hard way.

No doubt he would have asked about their relationship if he saw them being too close together because he was a very inquisitive Man.

Josh was almost reading that famous phrase in his mind just as Pete would ask why he would date an employee he was entrusted with to give training on the job to?

He knew the answer to that!

Josh had to find a way to distance himself from Kristy without drama on realizing his mistake, which came too quick than he would have wanted but now his job was on the line and he may just have to do the right thing, break up or move to another location.

The sad part was that he was falling in love with Kristy at the time. He feared he could lose his job for breaking work ethics, but now what next?

As for Kristy, it was one of those awkward moments so hard to come out of... She thought it was just a small fling and no commitments, but that is not how it went down. She actually wanted it to last, but since they had to deal with that situation, replacing Josh would be the next Step the pain she was feeling, she thought.

She went on a few dates but she didn't seem to meet the right guy, she thought Josh was that guy that would definitely put a ring on it, but not so fast!

Things turned upside down in her opinion!

Over time, she met this vibrant young and handsome man at a baseball game and they have been seeing each other a lot ever since they met, hopefully something better.

After josh explained to her they could not see each other any-more, she took it hard but on the other hand it was more like good riddance for Kristy now that she met this new guy who was just a lot of fun to be with!

By the look of it, she has changed much, no room for Josh even if he changed his mind about them.

He has to learn to stay away out of her way.

Josh on the other hand would have preferred to keep the relation-ship but for right now the job comes first until he figures out things, she may have met someone but he was only hoping on that old flame effect, that later on when everything is figured that there could still be some fire burning somewhere in Kristy's heart, she just had to wait a little longer, in this case, not for Kristy, she seemed to have moved on!

At the back of his mind, he hopes there's still a slim chance that somehow Kristy realizes that he still had feelings for her.

It's been a couple of months and It seemed Christy and Lance, the new man in her life were trying to nurture their relationship. She had this guy who was so excited to show her off to his friends, lavish din-ner, a camping trip just the two of them, breakfast in bed...

What more could she ask for?

who would have thought? She tells her friends about how She is so fascinated by him!

Things were looking pretty good for her.

A few months past, no doubt Josh was missing Kristy in his life, he complained literally about almost everything, from work to home then Friday watch game with friends and back to work... Things were getting stale... What a boring work life, he was beginning to turn himself into a grouchy young man!

Things happen but he didn't expect life to be like this,

Isn't it amazing that some women come into your life and it's all drama, while others, make you feel special? Debating in his mind... He knows better now.

Everything hurts, when he walks into a restaurant and, they just happen to play their favorite song which brings back the sad memories, that's not what he expected to feel after breaking up with her!

Josh turned to his friends for advice, he just couldn't stop thinking about her and the good times they shared together. Unfortunately, the friends weren't of much help either, both his friends told him to follow his heart, to hell with work ethics? Not so fast, that he can only tell his hurting 'Heart' but not his job, his friends told him!

Like every alpha male, he did not want to look like he was the weak one here, only he needed to tell someone how he felt or at least tell her!

He finally decided to go see her on his day off.

When he knocked at her door he was not sure what to expect but Kristy was happy to see him although he could tell that the reception wasn't the same, she was a little cold he did not get the French kiss and a warm hug as usual.

As he sat down, he realized she was watching a talk Show, obviously the situation was already tensed between them and everything was off, awkward silence was killing him, so he politely asked her to change to a sports channel after all her new boyfriend was a baseball player to which she accepted.

Josh pretended he wanted to catch up on some news he missed leaning back on the couch, he made a sigh Aahgh! That's better! She was filing her nails and didn't even look to his direction, she could have been thinking, what did he expect her to say?

He should never have shown up, at all, that was the look!

He thought, as they both sat in silence if only, he could hang on to his mission a little while and wait for a better moment to ask Kristy if she still had feelings for him because that would change things!

If that was the case, he was now willing to change his job title for things to work out between them and he was terribly sorry because he is now realizing that he was actually falling in love with her!

As he reached for the fridge to grab a drink, he saw that Kristy still kept his favorite drinks or was it just coincidence? This actually made him feel a little relieved, gaining courage, he asked Kristy how things were with Lance and if he should stop coming to her house and that at that moment he Just wanted to talk.

Don't ask such questions! I mean, don't you already know that I have someone in my life now but don't get me wrong we'll always be friends only I'm sorry, her voice faltered... Sounded more like she had some pain!

But now what? He was busy thinking if it was a bad idea to come to her house after all!

Moments later, Kristy ran to the bathroom crying, Josh rushed to her side too, giving her a much needed hug!

Oh! Please don't cry Josh told her, handing her some facial wipes!

He looked around and saw gifts he previously bought her sitting on the counter, he thought for a moment if Kristy was in love with the wrong guy and still wants him in her life but not quite from what she said or how she said it, he did not get it!

You still keep this? Holding the wooden box...

Yes! She answered.

There are some things you treasure and keep for long even after breaking up, you can't erase the sweet memories, would you? She asked Josh. Of cause not! He replied.

So there!

She said in a sarcastic way...

Don't have any emotions!

It's over Josh!

I keep everything that you gave me because they were gifts you gave to me out of love, I don't regret having met you, she told him.

Yes! I agree, and I meant every word engraved on that piece...

Mhm! I thought so, she replied.

Josh confirmed what his feelings were, but it's kind of a sticky situation they got themselves into and he hoped she understood his intentions, Meanwhile Josh had no idea why she was crying.

She had her fears too, she wished things were different, but things had changed between them, she told Josh! She had mixed feelings but at the same time she knew in her heart that she was falling in love with Lance, she could swear to her friends at work how he truly swept her off her feet but something seemed to bother her.

What is it Kristy?

Josh asked her but she was not talking to him moments passed, still blowing her nose...

What could possibly be wrong? He however broke the silence and apologized for coming to her house just to make her cry.

No, no! It's not you, waving her hands motioning him to sit down. She told him she had her own fears, getting caught between two men that she both likes but there's more to her breaking down!

It seems Lance did not get over his ex-girlfriend,

The calls between the two is driving her crazy and she still wondered if her and Josh could work things out!

Josh was shocked! That's exactly what he had hoped for, So she still can take him back after that selfish decision he made?

He was shaking his head!

Back to work, things seemed normal and he is a cool guy that would not just talk to anybody about his problems but to those that were very close to him and as a proud guy, he did not want to be seen to stoop too low or trying to beg. He had to tread very carefully and wanted Kristy to make up her mind and make the right decision.

Kristy Loves Lance to death, from what she has told her friends but she wants him to stop the phone calls to his ex-girlfriend every Friday night, whatever it was, it was ruining her whole weekend, she hopes that things would be good again.

As I talked to Josh he seemed distraught, but I assured him trying to make things feel a little less depressing, I can tell you this Josh, If Lance loved her as she claims, he needs to cut off every links he has with his ex-girlfriend in order for the new relationship he had with Kristy to work.

So, give it sometime things will be alright! You will meet someone else, I told him looking straight to his face.

meanwhile, he sat back, breathed a sigh of relief, thought for a moment then he lifted a little rubble that covered some wild flower near the bench we sat on and tossed it away!

whatever he had in mind at that moment he knew it alone…

I thought.

Tell you what? He finally spoke, I don't want to be between two people who love each other. I tried, it was a bad move, now I have to deal with it! He blurted out!

I had my chance and I blew it! He said reluctantly.

Thanks a lot, he told me.

Let's go in I think the boss is done with the meeting.

Josh said to me as he dropped a can of pop into the trash in style with both hands, a perfect throw as if to say, the hell with it!

If that brought relief to him, so be it!

I tilted my head as a sign to go, let's go in!

Yap! He said.

We both stood up and went back inside. Still a lot of tasks to cover before the day ends.

7
Objectives & Goals.

ANDRE IS BEING so impatient today, I thought it had to do with the survey conducted last week.

A lot of things were mentioned to be adjusted, it was going down!

Both the managers concerned were bracing themselves!

Not knowing what to expect. Andre was on top of his topic, he was pretty good at tough issues but he made sure changes were done with immediate effect!

I liked the way he does it, made me understand better issues of importance to the company. He majored in Economics & Administration but his skills could not be ignored Josh seemed to have recovered from his pain some, he had been very attentive during the meeting, talking of Andre's agenda, he leaned over to say something to me, the guy is smart, he whispered to me.

I thought so! I whispered back as I bent down to pick my pen to write certain details down.

Andre went on to talk about company's goals which included long term purposes which are generally qualitative. All activities should contribute to the firm's goals. Objectives are specific goals, specific targets for company's action with qualitative short time frames.

Objectives are always quantifiable and measurable to stimulate planning Ideas, business owners or stores like this one should study the firm's current market position, its strength and weakness. For us here the weakness could be shrink and incompetent employees.

We must ask ourselves what is the best way to go about it if faced with these situations.

Andre took a sip from his glass of water, probably his throat drying up due to covering many topics. As he continued to point out how to establish goals he drew out a project plan on the board.

No. 1. Target two or three specific objectives for the company.
2. Clear Analysis, possible strategies for achieving these objectives.
3. Select the course of action and develop a detailed action plan, develop also a criteria for measuring the company's progress towards its goals and objectives.
4. Analyse the structure of operation and evaluate if we are efficient.
5. prepare job descriptions,(accountability, Authority. etc.)
6. The need for a formal marketing plan.
7. Reliable data conduct market research.
8. Changes in market and competition, advertising and promotion, pricing and location.
9. We must remember that financial information system is the best defense against financial difficulties. It would be disastrous to ignore this because this is what brings even mighty companies down. Just as financial institutions would collect overdue accounts payable and take advantage of cash discounts to control costs, we too must clear out our inventory and minimize cash investments, stock controls and eliminate unprofitable products.
10. Good management is the key to consistent business success.

And lastly review plans periodically and revise when necessary and always remember to commit plan to paper and save on digital device for future follow up. We have made progress in the past weeks and I hope we will do better come the end of this season.

That's all folks, Andre said as he collected his files from the projector screen and left the room. Al' who was the operations manager, was seated at the front no doubt, he had a lot to put together.

Bob asked me if I wanted some coffee as he poured himself a cup, of course! I said, he leaned over a shelf to grab a bio-degradable paper Cup, he was big on saving the environment, I couldn't blame him...

Me being a germ freak, I hesitated for a moment before accepting the cup, just in case it wasn't a fresh cup! Sniffing through the aroma and breathing out... I sipped my coffee in silence for a moment enjoying the great taste of good coffee. Bob on the other hand, sipped his coffee too fast, that's when hunger calls or time to re-energize as we call it but he is a big boy he can handle it!

Al' walked over to our table.

Mmh... Thanks to the never drying pot of coffee.

Okay, man, enjoy it! Just what you need at this particular time, Bob responded.

Good idea, I said. Work had been stressful to most department heads that week, keeping up with changing systems and beating the odds!

Ads were printed out yet the products were not readily available due to bad weather, since the ads were already out for the week, they just had to find a way to deal with the glitch, guests angry for the wrong information printed on weekly Special, guests rely on this just to find exactly what they are looking for and know the prices beforehand.

It was hard to deal with a tight situation but Al' being the genius that he was, he turned things around knocking off at least 10% off a similar product to these guests, who were at the time very disappointed for time wasted but later, all smiles after their needs were met.

All he cared about was a guest walking out of the door happy because he believed word of mouth was very powerful, if the company portrays a good image, it reflects back and was beneficial for business.

8
Meeting the Tasks.

BOB AND I have been working on the grill displays building decks to fit what we had chosen to attract sales for almost one hour when we saw Andre' haul up empty boxes, obviously a sign of delayed merchandise not brought to sales floor on time.

Andre' was that kind of person who believed in ' do it yourself' I was not surprised to see him get his hands dirty. He must have been working on something serious earlier Bob mentioned that to me.

I guess so!

I replied back.

Brenda had a lot to do today after organizing her departments, she had to help with structures and the decor plans. Marisa the manager in charge of this department Was so far deep into the creative art, no doubt, obviously, the guest members consulting with her, experienced great satisfaction because she did her own follow ups just to make sure the members did the right thing after leaving the store, that exclusive attention was a welcome gesture that's what I would say, good for business!

There's no better way to describe the feelings of an investor after he sees his numbers rising, whatever it takes, most investors are willing to take risks, I mean Informed ones!

Marisa is no push over, she is the type that would not go away until she gets a proper answer to her question by that I mean, work related issues, looking at me directly he said don't have ideas!

Of course not!

I was just listening to you, quite interesting to be precise I don't know her that much, I met her once at the boardroom and I think it was her first attendance if I remember, she didn't talk much.

She was about ten feet away still talking to one of the club members. She understood that people everywhere Irrespective of where they were or who they were, they required full attention and proper explanation about a product they were about to purchase, she was good at that, I mean top notch!

I quickly read her name tag and said Hi, she replied back.

Hi! And you are? Ah... Making it hang... Not knowing my name.

To avoid that awkward moment I pointed at my Name tag so she gets it right!

Oh, right! Short name, she said! I try to make it easy so you don't have to suffer, right?

Pronunciation never comes out right, especially a hard name to read!

She just smiled to my joke and did not say anything more about it! I've heard about you!

you are the.... Nodding my head confirming that she knew my position, I said Yes! To save her from unnecessary information, she didn't need at the time.

We are coming over to help you as soon as I replace this lever on this grill, Bob said to her.

Okay, I'm waiting! She said as she started to walk away towards her department.

We had to join in and help her, this was a major project! We had to in-corporate a new concept with the already established line in the department, Marisa's expertise was required at this point, however this meant we had to temporarily abandon what we were doing.

Bob had a way of saying things, you couldn't turn him down. I was dragging my feet over to the other side of the store. Hey, it was hard to refuse to help out, this was a genuine project especially her? She gets things done and to that, I'd like to support that kind of spirit!

Bob was assertive when it comes to things like this!

Let's get to work guys, Bob Calling on to the other employees who were to help out but were still standing around waiting for instructions.

As it turned out it wasn't too bad after all looking at the before and after? Big difference!

Job well done!

Finally we finish the project and back to our unfinished project where we had to fix a cardboard both sides of the display. He wanted to put a mark on where the borders would end but the markers he had in his pocket apparently had ran out Of ink, as he tried each and every one of them dropping the very dry ones on an empty box he brought with him.

Not good! He exclaimed!

Dropping a bunch of them into the box, he usually says this is for any other eventuality, good idea.

Keep the trash where it belongs before fully disposing of them, not the floor, he says. I came to his rescue having some myself clipped to my work file.

I never want to waste time! He said that to me, he was getting frustrated after walking around the shelves and making a decision, I guess it takes a lot to get everything right he asked me to cross the old price on the grills and write by hand the new price using the markers in his hands, I did just that!

Sales gimmicks, I thought. It's what meets the eye that triggers the brain to make the decision to either buy it or skip it!

In other words People are convinced more to buy if the price fits their budget. Companies must think seriously about the quality of the brands they display. I had to register this in my mind because we expect to do this again come the next season.

I thought Bob was a bright man but also on the other hand I wondered about his rebellious side where you had to listen to what he had to say even if you thought he was way out of line!

The good part, he was quick to apologize, even better, over a glass of scotch!

He was too nice of a person to hurt a fly.

I guess everything has its own balance, including human beings!

9
In stock Tasks.

AFTER WE FIXED the last Top shelf, I had to finish some of my work on screen, advertising was tough, getting illustrations the way it remains attractive on a glossier bonded paper, color separation and more, man you have to get it right!

That's every tutor's slogan!

The employer does not want to see failures but I'm glad my graphics class helped me to learn the tricks and I can proudly say that I'm driven towards excellence!

By creating the final finish with such finesse, I count the many hours of toil but I still give credit to my ever demanding tutor, a man who was never satisfied with a finished product until he pins it on a bright light fixture on the wall judging every detail of the print.

I swear the long spell while waiting for his approval just sent chills to every student! Even if it was a fairly good work, there are Moments you doubt yourself as for him, he enjoyed the suspense because pushing a student to the limits only proved to him about a good outcome.

A few times, I had to wait patiently before I could hear him mumble, Aah... Very nice! So I pick up my finished work and storm out of the class Phew! Jeez! Sometimes I wonder why people have to try and find faults even though they know there's none!

One of my colleagues always bluffs that if the experts couldn't tell his flaws then his work piece was pretty good!

Scratching my head to settle on what will fit correctly With the season's theme, selecting each piece and comparing, thinking I still had to complete and present the finished piece to Andre' and the rest of the team before the final print, I had to make up my mind and time was running out!

The last on my list, was to check on Phillip and max at the adjacent warehouse within the store's premises...

All merchandise lands at this particular area and it was more like their domain!

Unique thing, they both share the love of sports but had constant arguments over various things ranging from scores of their favorite teams to almost anything!

Phillip born in Mexico but raised in the United States, his Mexican accent was lost somewhere, his Spanish was bad, you could only hear him speak Spanish with his mother, Last time I saw them together was when she needed supplies for her 'cinco de' mayo 'May fifth' Celebrations treat for her friends and family, Phillip didn't understand it and so the revolution dates had very little meaning to him.

No offence! Phillip would say but Younger generation like me don't know about it and may not relate well with it, they just know that fifth of May has some meaning to the old folks...

A fine young man who knew his job self-motivated. Both him and Max worked hard to cope with the demand before them. His love for soccer was great, while Max had love for Baseball. He played for his team back in Atlanta, Georgia.

When they couldn't make it to the world series, no doubt his dream fell through but he remained a loyal New York Yankees fan.

While I was approaching their work area, I couldn't help but hear their arguments, complaining about the back breaking Job they had to do that afternoon. Phillip commented that the work involved was a lot, and they could not meet the deadline, and so more help would mean, merchandise moving quickly to sales floor and we can make some good sales at a required time frame.

when I suggested a fork lift to help move some of the heavy merchandise, he corrected me, Oh No! This 'Amigo'

knows only licensed crew can handle such machinery he should have briefed you.

Oh really? I was shocked, they were not licensed!

So you too can't handle it? Yes! They replied almost at the same time.

Point taken, I told them.

I will mention this to Al' so he can do something about it. I got a little concerned and listed the situation for the next Boardroom agenda, delayed merchandise to sales floor, so not acceptable!

I asked them, if they had discussed this with their Supervisor, to which to which the answer was yes. And I was surprised, he didn't do anything about it!

But what happened? I asked.

Hiring freeze! They told me Meanwhile, we continue to do the job five people combined would still feel the burden, max said that painfully...

Oh that's sad, I said.

Okay, I will suggest to Al' to bring other employees to come and help for today's delivery. No, tomorrow Philip corrected me.

Al' knows what Urgency means, so I know he will solve the problem for you guys soon enough, meanwhile let's focus on what needs to be done now. Okay, they agreed.

I stuck around to help to which they both appreciated, Well done guys!

I told them as we cleared the last box.

You can go home, it's way past your clock out time.

Max is the type that does not talk much when Working, I don't blame him, concentration is required at this point. While in second grade, he fell from the playground swing and injured his eardrum, he lost hearing completely on the right side of his ear so the hearing aid has been of great help to him.

He appreciates how tiny they make them these days so he doesn't have to wear it from outside his earlobe but inside and he can adjust the volume by simply touching a button which came in handy when machinery was in action creating noise preventing him to hear Philip, his work buddy.

No doubt, he made fun of him too because sometimes he could hear perfectly well but instead made his buddy raise his voice when in conversation with him.

Wiping dust off his pants, he told me they got help earlier in the day, unfortunately, they were called back too soon, busy weekend, he said.

I guess this extra information was to tell me he was not accusing his supervisor directly.

That's good if there was help even if for a short time, I told him. Leaving the room, behind me, I could hear Philip yell at Max, we need these items separated, are you deaf? He asked Max Max was not amused with the comment. He fired back!

Deafness! You know nothing about it because you are not!

Talking of being deaf, I will tell you about my uncle who was previously deaf but regained his hearing, he played being deaf still, for what reasons we did not know yet.

Max continued to explain.

My uncle found out about assumingly private conversation between his closest relatives, he heard one and all the conversations, no doubt he changed his will several times. So don't ask me if I'm deaf because it wasn't my choice!

I can tell the difference, he said defiantly!

And by the way completely deaf people read lips, I don't !

Wow!

That's quite a story Philip said.

Sorry if I went too far.

Friends?

Extending his hands to Max…

yeah, friends! Max responded, sorry I snapped! He apologized to his friend, don't do that again!

I stepped back to find out what the yelling was about, they were back working but I still had to ask why Max raised his voice so loud, I could hear him from the entrance…

What's going on? I asked.

Oh no, Phillip is my buddy we graduated from the same high school, we just have some differences but at the end of the day he gives me a ride home, my wife's car was scratched pretty bad and it's still at the body shop so she is using my car, she never found out who did it till today yet she has parked at the same spot for a couple of years, really well lit designated parking area at her work place.

I don't get it how some irresponsible person like that would go un noticed!

I expect this kind of acts around stadiums, where there's crowd after a game. Like my brother his car was full of dents always after the games, I still remember one player who had great performance, my brother's favorite team, made twenty home runs, two hundred and fifty at tacks.

A few people could not match his numbers, my brother enjoyed being in the crowd, he explained! That's how he got his car dinged most of the time but a few years later he decided he was tired of the many repairs, expensive cars are not cheap to repair.

The new stadium is so different at present, it's not the 1943 stadium anymore, broadcast is better, better cameras, viewing in HD is as good as being there yourself so my brother resorted to watching from his large screen at home, Max explained.

Anyway guys, this is a work place we've got to keep our voices down, Okay? I told them.

Looking back at each other as if to gain approval, yes, thank you! They replied back. As far as that feud was concerned, my advice was enough. They are great young men, I would only be concerned If it got out of hands then I will need to report the incident but as for now, I heard nothing and my lips are sealed!

10
Get it done.

IT WAS BREAK time, Al' and me sat out on the wooden bench which was exposed to the sunny side of the store. He preferred that side to the hard concrete which a group of friends would sit during their break from the busy work place, as they like to say a minute out to clear the head.

I don't know about that, all I know is that anybody would enjoy a break whether your head clear or not!

Al' has tried to stop smoking in vain, he recently enrolled in a program, hopefully to help him quit for good!

More often than not, he admitted to sabotaging his efforts by not taking the first step!

So the program in place, he just joined will help him a great deal Al' had to do his two puffs before he said a thing tilting his head facing up and blowing that smoke away from his face in satisfaction.

It was like a sacred thing he had to do after a tough day and doing some math that was impossible to solve!

All the same he did his job anyway. His style? Who knows! Maybe it's an earned experience! He looked to my side as I tried to pop a can of soda, thank God, these days it's not just any type of soda but you can make wise choices like sugar free which comes in different flavors!

I try to comfort myself that way when I intentionally plan to cheat on my diet, I mean not always but once in a while.

If excuses are not accepted, then I've got to blame it on someone, I thought!

These days it is almost a crime to talk about soda!

Huh! All the calories? You mean you still drink soda?

I was asked once! I almost said to her, you have no business in what I eat but instead I just remained polite. My answer to her was, yap!

In my head, I was satisfied that I had control of what I eat and regulate what goes through my mouth by choice, as far as I was concerned, I was doing just fine and I didn't need some self-appointed nutritionist who had no known records of the other healthy meals that I normally eat.

I sipped my soda as I relaxed my feet trying to lift them up a little before finally resting them on the ground. I was looking towards the group across us to see if I knew any of them but before I made any comment. Al' said something to me that I did not expect, putting his cigarette away and blowing the last puff he said to me those, Pointing at them.

They are the back stubbing group!

I mean, based on evidence, not just saying we have lost great employees after certain issues ensured coming from this group of people, they have been given a second chance, meaning we expect better.

I was rather surprised but he cautioned me, don't be!

Remember, you can't change people unless they themselves do so! What a shame!

It's such a setback when you think you are on the same pace but you find out the hard way that you are not!

But tell you what? If they want to leave for another occupation, you can't stop them either but it would be a welcome solution.

Sometimes people like that move from job to job because they can't keep up with company policies.

I know, I replied So we have to keep hiring until we find the one willing to stay and build a career here, for those new employees who may not find what they are looking for at this particular environment, you can go ahead and say, they have no place here and most times they are gone in a heartbeat!

Those welcome to stay are the ones that have the potential and take seriously the company's policies into consideration!

Time and money wasted? Not what you want to be the norm but rather work hard to reduce it! So think about it! You want to hire who can work and blend in with the environment!

Don't get me wrong, I'm not against hiring but I do believe in keeping experienced workers who can deliver and keep the company running, hire more if necessary and make changes when there's need not because we do not to be that company that can't keep their employees due to bad management but won't keep those with bad intentions.

And may I ask why you think there's some bad apple?

His answer to me was, negligence!

Regulations are set but are the rules kept?

In my mind I'm thinking who regulates the regulators?

He went on to say, these are the managers that wouldn't do their job right, lack of Professionalism, no proper work ethics, but quick to write bad publicity on anyone better than them and will always try to shift the blame to loyal employees under them.

Un necessary threats that does not make sense and never spending time to know the good employees, they have to learn and know what these employees strengths are, how they can be utilized better and what they are capable of doing in terms of the company's growth but instead these managers act like some motorized device.

Oh! Not so in this kind of industry, one has to be more practical to bring it on!

In most cases you will find that these types of managers do not have better communication skills and you wonder how they got the position in the first place!

However what you will find is that they delegate more than necessary and participate in very little projects.

your company is going down if you have these kind of managers! Small company owners may not know but they do exist... Some were employed right from college no prior retail or marketing experience except for what they learnt in class. To create a base, such tend to favor some who fall under their wings or those who agree with them for some reason and less favor to those who did not agree with them.

Equal opportunity employer?

Yeah, right!

Think again only professionals respect that!

Oh really? How about good looks? I asked him?

Good looks are important too, depending on what you are selling!

Oh, I see your reaction!

Leaning against the wall facing me and talking directly, to me in a low tone, he asked as if to make a point using his fore finger, why do most employers invest more on employees?

The answer to that is simple, long serving employees do not require further training if not just for updates on certain matters but rather they would willingly share knowledge with the new employees. This is expected to enhance good work ethics. And also performance of older employees is considered consistent in every way that's the way I look at it, he said.

I could see a smile at the corner of his mouth still emphasizing his point.

I cleared my throat to agree with him in some way but he still continued...

If I say the beauty of having responsible employees, I don't just mean beauty but good representation, neat and not looking clumsy! If an employee is beautiful or handsome, that's a plus too but not a ticket to get a job, in this case we need brains not just looks!

Hmm... Thinking aloud!

yeah, I remember certain companies that I know of, where you can literally see that the employee is overworked and underpaid, representation is so poor but even for those who try, you could see that they are living a passive life! And more so, they'd like to shove you off and just finish the work at hand and go home!

It's almost like the employee is saying to you, if you do not get great customer service, in case you did not know 'I'm here to get my bills paid, not all of them because I'm paid peanuts! Other than that, this company sucks!

Al' was waiting to see if the information he just told me resonated with me in some way!

I just nodded, meaning I understood, but we could do better than those alleged companies!

I have mentioned this several times during a board meeting so we don't fall into that trap. Talking of companies out there, a lot of times you would find that the system is so messed up that the top office overlooks the important part and that is what can bring a great business down.

what I mean by that, is all these employees want to be treated with respect even though they might have their own issues but think about it, after all the training, you want to keep them, believe it or not consumers want knowledgeable employees who can help them quick enough and they'd be out of there back to their own business, save their time and yours it obviously helps the company project more on customer experience!

Al' mentioned that to me he was watching my body language, how I would react!

Twitching a little bit, a way to ease things up, I do understand your point! I said to him.

At least I try not to suck at my job but do it right!

Al', cutting me short making sure I did not misunderstand him in some way, he briefly said we'll leave it at that!

I must say he is a down to earth fellow very inspiring, his advices are sure to encourage, I think it's to do with his past, having been a fire fighter, he lost two of his best friends to an inferno that swept the better part of southern California around the so called 'the rich neighborhood' if you get what I'm saying…

He says he has no regrets, he did what he did for the love of life and making a difference in people's lives.

The only regret he has today as he describes it, is to associate with those people who refuses or has no interest to learn from the experts to perfect their skills!

He says he was only made stronger when that fierce fire engulfed his two friends as he watched helplessly from a closer ridge he says they miscalculated the depth of the fire and went in only to be surrounded by the flames completely surrounding them it was a bad scene and a bad experience on the job, he said.

He realizes that he has a good reason to live, he appreciates every breath he has today, he also knows that it's important to inspire others, to help them improve their lives to become better people, better ideas plant a good seed in others not scorn!

That was the best way he could say it say it, either way, I was okay with his advice!

11
Boardroom.

THE LORD IS gracious! I thought to myself after hearing Al's close brush with death! That after noon, I sat at the back of the lounge not wanting to say a thing but to just listen to what others had to say Al' had a departmental meeting with the supervisors, I could tell they had several recommendations for the boardroom this coming as I waited patiently for him to finish that meeting.

I watched how he conducted that meeting with authority, there and then I knew he had some special qualities.

On realizing what friends or work mates can be accepting them as they are, weak or strong from my thought, we all have special qualities in some way or the other.

I could not leave without him because we had some work to finish before the end of the day. I could hear him give several notes including codes, they would automatically know which zone was doing its best in meeting daily goals, he went on as the meeting progressed!

He knew how to address his team and to get important but hard to solve issues out and on the list ready just in time for the next boardroom for every member to discuss.

He went on to tell his team that this type of company will need at least several hours to monitor certain merchandise sales, increase and more so after the stock market closes gets feedback of total review for the day. The analysis will show what was lost and the reasons and how to keep watch on shrinkage at all costs!

He looked across the room as if to identify someone in particu-lar, but continued talking by saying cashiers must identify mark down items and what has not been marked down because labels have been switched before by some dishonest people, you never know who it is until it's investigated, it is the job of the cashier handling the prod-uct to verify if the numbers of reduced price merchandise matches if not, they know what to do in a polite way but seek the help of a supervisor.

I'm speaking broadly on every situation here, he said!

In a branch big as this one, you can't miss those employees who may be tempted to be dishonest for whatever reasons, I don't know but I want to believe there is none because most of them have proven to be what we expected them. Passing the 'E-verify' process was great but staying on the job is what matters.

Even though there might not be. Any bad Apple at the moment but just look out for any discrepancies, they may try to mark down items which are not listed to clear for their benefit or to others known to them, not new?

Absolutely!

Others have tried to do exactly that only to regret later. The out-look is important and that made it necessary to put in place a system that could validate items quickly.

so the current updating systems obviously made a difference, it picks out what type of merchandise is not in the correct category in terms of pricing and set up. The company must keep watch for any pitfalls, I will say that again today as a reminder.

I'm saying this out of experience, don't quote me wrong it has hap-pened before it can still happen if we do not do our jobs right but so far we have not seen any suspicious case but it can happen so we must be on the lookout at all times why because you work here it should mean something to you !

Got it! I said.

That little help is not little after all, if it can stop shrinkage and help our sales to increase. If we get enough profits employees can be awarded a share of the profits. Some seasons accelerated more profits, while others did not depending on the market sales and seasons but changing with the trend must be in the plan always!

Another thing we have to look into, we must constantly keep our facility clean, the daily cleaning charts shows you as a supervisor how many times the floor has been cleaned, but there are issues of spills, litter when we are constantly busy.

If this is the case when you are the supervisor on duty you must advice employees concerned accordingly or just do the right thing, you all know what I mean by that! Al' said. We must keep the facility clean.

The survey we conduct has been more frequent than before why? There's more competition than ever this is done to guide us and to help keep our track records. We must stay on top of things in retail business, a lot of things can go wrong!

One :- Our performance in sales...

Two :- How are we rated in the market place? We have to be proud that our name has stayed on top in this region, he said it with pride.

We were not named on top of the chart in this region for nothing? We worked so hard to bring it to that level even though we are only a few years old, we earned it!

I could hear everybody roaring...

Yay! Yes! Sure, big one still coming!

The team was fired up! That's what I'm talking about!

Al' sealed It!

You want to know something? This resonates with me because I understand how hard work pays I told Al'.

People who anticipate growth, only they knew how or when they reached their peak season. Decision makers depended on the outcome report specifically that's why under normal Circumstances, they are a little reserved not to reveal what the situation really is!

Al' gave them the speech they had wanted to hear in a long time, a joke or two to keep on their faces then he went on to say that we'd like to do better next time, so far for this zone, we are ranked the best choice by the previous survey in terms of customer service and productivity amongst other retailers, not bad at all!

This we must also remember to appreciate our associates who are productive, look at their performance the charts, how can we motivate them. Andre' joined the meeting when Al' was almost closing his meeting.

Supervisors aired their views, most of the them were demands which to my thinking, Al would prefer to endorse to boardroom.

Recognizing the Branch manager amidst claps and cheering, Al' handed the mike to Andre, as usual Andre greeted the supervisors and listened to their views.

Andre' explained to the managers that some of the issues discussed will be recommended in the next boardroom, excusing himself to attend an urgent matter, he agreed to meet them at the members club after the a baseball tournament his son was playing at seasons finals is coming Sunday, his son was one of the best players, so this was a major event for Andre', he had to be there for him, he had that re-assuring feeling that his son was going to do great and that he should worry about nothing, but focus more on his performance.

The young man was in good shape and geared for this particular game, He couldn't be more proud!

I asked Al' why he had to talk about official matters out of office...

He chuckled and looked me straight in the eye and said here, we get our work done no matter where we are if the information was required to see the success we both expect!

We have particular company strategies and regulations, these meetings are only to benefit our work for this branch and everything we discuss is strictly confidential.

By the way, those laptops supervisors carry along with them were provided by the company to have the work done.

Understandably, with laptops managers can work from any location to have your work done so are we good?

Yeah, I said.

It's always hard to access your PC when you have to be on sales floor but only after the hustle and bustle so that's why we came up with buying enough laptops for our supervisors and department managers so far it has worked and produced good results.

The slim I pads enables you all to do and have work done at appropriate time so it's up to those who are willing to work with me or decide not to but at boardroom, I need results!

No kidding! Someone in the background, shouted!

Al', certainly knew how to play his part so well even in difficult situations surrounding retail business, this includes those yelling and displeased clients, the never Satisfied type no matter how you explain the situation.

He says, give it your best short! Meaning? Don't react in a similar way as the complainant!

As one of the top managers, he had his techniques which just got down so well with his staff.

I could remember when he had to give support to a safety program organized by the local community, handling issues intelligently was the key thing in his memo. He had to give assistance to two of a special operation team placed to work as cashiers to help trace some drug lords seen in the neighborhood and had had terrorized all kinds of people.

The project was later documented as a very successful mission.

These criminals used fake identity cards during transactions most probably, to hide their true identities with a mission to steal or conceal information.

How they stole this credit cards, social security numbers could not be immediately established, they were getting a lot smarter than you would think, no traces on social media but what this team found out was a hard nut to crack, they used codes no one could de-code, their website and the crime was spreading much to the frustration of the local Authorities.

When the intelligence bracket tried in vain, not able to crack through that web, it became apparent that it was already so hard to connect the dots that would lead to arrests.

The local police chief presented his plan on how to tackle the issue, his suggestion was hard to embrace but if executed well could work.

His request to business owners to cooperate was his idea of making the operation to succeed he said netting out those crooks involved would mean the communities must participate too to help beat these guys on their own master plans.

So the saying is, with all the spiked up info lines, cell phones wire taps, even an ear to the ground, informants included but information like this one was always hard to close in to, it takes time to be acted upon because it wasn't just the criminals but also in consideration of the civilians that could be affected!

So what's the deal? Swift move might help, or it will be too late, busting out smarter guys like these ones!

So as things went by so I heard, local intelligence made some head way reaching the house these criminals briefly stayed two days after they already left for another location, another set back!

12
The Landlord.

SWENSON WAS INNOCENT landlord, he rented out the house to people he thought were very honest from the way they conducted themselves he said they sounded and looked very professional they paid his rent on time sometimes four months in advance, he had no reasons to suspect anything. As Swenson pulled up the driveway, the cops thought he was one of the suspects returning home, seeing all the three cop cars parked across his drive way, he nearly tripped wondering what it could be?

He heard the cops call to him to stop! Get down on the ground! Things happened so fast, he was tongue tied!

The daily instructions were ringing in his ear and he had to just follow what they said to him to put hands over his head!

One of the officers shouted at the top of his voice telling him to turn around!

Did he have a choice? Of course not!

He obeyed and turned around facing the wall but too shaken to speak…

The officer approached him and as usual he was quickly pinned down to the ground! At the corner of his eye, he saw the hand cuffs dangling ready to be clipped on both his hands.

He felt he was getting breathless, what's happening? What have I done to deserve this? He asked!

Just shut up! Snarled the cop, quite a big guy, shoved him around before saying anything to him!

Read him his Miranda rights!

Someone in the crowd shouted, because of the abrupt activity in the neighborhood with sirens going off, a crowd had just formed right in front of the condominiums that Swenson owned a few units at! Surprisingly enough, a lot of people on the ground knows a lot about common laws and you can't take them for a ride, like the guy who just made his voice heard, he didn't need to go to any Law school to know that!

You have the right to remain silent, what you say can be used against you, he knew the rest of it but had to obey whatever they said to him.

In his mind he was being cooperative, he thought.

What the hell is this?

Apparently, there's very little you can do to get all the answers you seem to ask in a case of mistaken identity like this one, you have to remain patient.

They took everything out of his pocket reading his Identification card very closely.

No piece of paper was left in his pocket, luckily some receipts played a big role leading to the cuffs being taken off his wrist. He was not the guy they were looking for but the information he had could be helpful!

A receipt of a door replacement kit his tenants required the previous month. Sometimes I wonder why men in general keep so many receipts in their wallets instead of a book keeping folder if in business? But so far it worked for Swenson!

Swearing… un cuff me! Jeez, You already know I'm not Your guy! They were shocked to find out he was not their guy, found nothing of interest in his car and set him free. He was fairly shaken, Swenson was ready to co-operate if his help was needed…

Unfortunately not a lot of luck in this instance since his previous tenants did not use their real names when signing the rental contract!

The names used were totally different on the contract so chances were slim but as they say any little information can help in some leads if not at all!

Swenson was shocked to hear that criminal activities actually occurred at his exclusive condominium which he crafted with special specification, befitting for a high profile business man or woman of style and a great neighborhood only for high society!

During further search, same prepaid phone with no name attached to it was used to call Swenson to collect his keys was found hanged on one of the hooks inside the garage kind of neat, come to think about it, they cared about the house and Swenson, only he did not need to meddle in their affairs!

What do we get from this act?

The only thing I can think of, is that these people were so smart and planned on not being traced!

During the search for any clue, they found no cutlery mainly plastic plates, paper plates and cheap serviettes, no beddings, three campers flat air mattresses on the floor, cleaned trash can. That was enough evidence they were not coming back. The chief knew he could execute the job and bring the criminals to book with the help of his team. Special operations group were positioned at different cities within the affected states.

The chief was hopeful because he had his best men out there, a good cropped up plan and time was the issue, only time!

He said to his officers as he gave instructions on his next move.

The survey took more than a month, the chief was getting impatient, but his plan was to hire his men who would work at strategic points, some were cashier slash undercover cops transmitted by cordless pin clipped on top of the ear contour insulated to protect the skin contact but had pointer heads on both ends, hidden from sight, they also used pin camera's for close face capture.

The criminals tried every trick and it worked for them for a while before being caught! From my understanding, they were not like the typical bank robber, they had very smooth techniques, never been caught how they operated was puzzling!

After robbing a few banks, they could almost get away with everything!

A bank teller would rather give out the money than lose their own life. Last scenario was almost like they used the help of a professional choreographer!

They hit several banks, amount of time spent each time, less than ten minutes and out of the door with the loot, makes you wonder if some inside job took place but after investigations, it seemed more they are acting only within their web.

If the card issuer has been informed of the loss of the card, no transaction by these criminals can be successful but the truth is, the affected party finds out after card has been used and the damage has been done!

The chief's comments favored chipped cards to non-chipped ones because he thought it could delay this act, these guys are always a plan a head.

People affected reported their cards missing, nothing else stolen from their cars at a secured parking lot and some cards were connected to missing persons or were already dead, yet the cards were fully functional, someone had to stop this!

The Chief said.

The way these crimes committed were so similar the style was shocking!

As we learnt later, these criminals were on the edge,

simply do not stand on their way or get wiped out !

The neighbors interviewed thought the opposite about Swenson's former tenants!

They said those neighbors were friendly and looked to be very nice people, played with kids in the neighborhood they were just like normal people nobody could suspect anything! Before the interview by the local authorities ended, these neighbors requested respect for their privacy, and I'm left thinking!

Are they them?

I guess we'll never know how extensive the spider web was!

Their phones or voicemails had no pointers, if they had theft deals, they never said it on the phones or they used codes hard to crack!

13
Community support.

DELIBERATIONS WERE MADE but in order to make that project successful, Al' and all the members of management had to conceal the identity of these two undercover personnel, to the rest, they were just new employees.

Troy one day found Steve giving a coded message sitting at the back of his car, he must have been shocked to see all the gadgets in Steve's car.

He stood back for a moment, Creepy... He thought!

Steve may not be his real name, people are bright not only in America but around the globe, he could be another member of secret service who knows!

He wondered. He was close but it was none of those!

A lot closer to home that's what it was!

Of course, Troy was right in away but our lips were sealed. Hey are you creating some computer game or something? He approached Steve... Naa, just like electronic stuff! He said Steve could not reveal his identity so instead he cracked a joke about some football commentator... They both laughed, how funny that was!

Steve and his mate worked together joked with these cashiers hoping no one blows his cover, Steve wanted this done sooner than later, from his reports he was highly skilled and could speak seven foreign languages fluently. You could not tell if he was born in Spain or Mexico.

His accent, too perfect! If he said hey my friend !

He sounded more like a true 'castellano, a Spanish dialect spoken in regions like Catalonia, Valencia and Balearic islands although you would expect this trick to be hard on Steve but he understood which generation he was speaking to, meaning words and translations meant totally different things between certain ages! His heavy accent changed from language to language but he knew how to blend it all, a stepped up tone through his nose and loosened tongue. He was good at it!

Adio`s, Amigo! He told the guest who was Hispanic male. Adio`s! The guest said back to him and left.

Spanish, that's how you speak it! He bragged about it! He was even better on green day, which of cause is St Patrick's day he said 'Slainte mhath' to Irish guests that passed through his line. They were obviously pleased to reply back.. Pronounced 'Slancha Vah' which simply means' In your good health'.

After his short shift he had another office to report to, chief! The job had to be done he had to get down to his computer download all that he thought was as suspicious transactions, matched the pictures On records, the data base is voluminous but worth keeping, records of repeating offenders was scary. Criminals previously busted, care less about What's next but what they can get away with!

It took several weeks to perfect his new position, he saw sex offenders who he tried to find but could not.

He felt a tight knot in his belly when he saw one of the guys he had been looking for staring right at his face during a transaction, he never moved a muscle.

He was amazed how patience took the better part of him, the way he did not lose his temper but he comforted himself that it's all about the techniques to use and good skills.

He had to pretend to hug at least one of the most wanted guys, he put a little transmitting button between his fingers and approached the guest, good to see you again man! He said putting his finger to work in style, patting him on his upper shoulder positioning the button where it's not noticeable!

Steve made a sigh of relief, mission accomplished!

We all know the feeling, I thought!

At least one case is close to being solved part of his job was done here, the fellow will be transmitting everywhere he goes without knowing but his team had to move fast after the lead!

The team was able to track the particular criminal tracing his every move through out until he hang his blazer him well throughout the day. To Steve the wheel had started rolling, they could not delay any further. Steve laughed at the idea of certain movies where a good guy has to play a bad guy just to reach his mission, as for him he played quite the opposite in his mind he knew he was just doing his job but only at a different location.

Steve, back to his desk, he scanned through the data base, new details he found made him proud of his most recent discovery that afternoon.

Apparently the same man he managed to place a transmitting button on, had other criminal records including rape, kidnapping, burglary and in possession of un licensed weapon.

How he could be just walking the streets, playing games with the cops and not being caught for that long?

He asked himself?

Steve recalled, they could not trace his DNA even with the latest technology available at special labs for criminal cases.

The DFY 5 only helped trace each individual criminal after being booked for the offence which was way overdue for a charge, this made it difficult to trace those criminals who clean up evidence after committing a crime but Steve meant business and vowed to help get these guys out of the streets and send them where they belong. behind bars.

If they have been rehabilitated, well and good but as for now he is not leaving any stone unturned!

This was one of a kind, an exceptional case, it was sad they could not find him even after he left evidence behind to tell the cops who he was.

Although this type of criminal was wise enough not to leave anything that could match his DNA samples after rape in case he was caught but Steve and the chief was hopeful all along that one day soon they will get him 'you can't run away from the long arms of the Law, he said this to his colleague many times.

The chief had a televised conference talking of what plans he had for the residence of this particular city and together with his team he strongly believed that this type of criminal activity can be eliminated and the man in question should not be left out another day especially knowing what he was capable of doing, he was set to do his job and stay connected, he did exactly that.

During this operation Steve saw all types of clues he needed but when he finally got some details that led to arrest of one of the drug lords, he called the chief and gave him his plan of action, the backup team ready I knew you could do it, he said from the other end, they can't be smarter than the current technology we have, the chief encouraged Steve.

That was more like the chief! Steve smiled and closed his laptop drinking his last cup of coffee. It's time to crack down on the bad guys Talking to himself but loud enough for his colleague to hear, glued to his work, he nodded in agreement to what Steve said he did not need to look up because he understood what that meant.

When the rest of the staff heard about the news, everyone who knew about the operation was rushing to the lounge to watch more about it.

I looked at Steve's picture on the news flash on TV screen about the good work they did I knew their job was done at our premises, he deserved that honor.

The, cartel was disbanded leaving most of the group members behind bars. The new technology has been more helpful today than it was years ago, Steve comparing to what they were able to do to get these guys.

In my mind I was thinking if I was in that position of Steve, having a criminal staring at me, I would bust him right away and stop wasting more time, may be not, that was unprofessional thought!

In this case, there were lives of unsuspecting guests, Steve's way was the best, I thought! Apparently the team's style was not to create any suspicion plus they considered safety of the customers inside the shops, most of these criminal carry guns with them, any commotion was to be avoided by all means, that is why experienced cops know they must use caution in a case where kidnapping was involved, anything could happen and things can change in a snap!

If the cop makes any stupid mistake, the victim can be shot to death, no doubt back at where Steve temporarily worked, there was joy and celebration after finding out his true identity, to them he was the hero they want to associate with but to their disappointment, Steve was no longer at the station but deployed elsewhere after his big promotion, a touch with the media and some death threat leaf lets and a marriage proposal from a fan who just found out who he was, she had a 'thing' for the men in blue!

Although gun laws are strict at the moment, it does not stop these criminals from buying, AR's, machine guns and other deadly weapons are still readily available, if not at the Gun shops, black market business is still thriving underground.

Cowboy states, any adult can be licensed to own a gun and to most it's considered fashionable! Most sales occur in the streets and gun shows same as buying ammunitions, AR's 223,357 magnum,45 Auto, the list is long young starters always try 22 long rifle either at the range or open desert, they have to keep up with the family tradition with guns passed over from generation to generation this however grants them the cowboy and cowgirl status as they adapt to the outdoor lifestyle!

Here in the East coast, you'd be lucky to have your gun in one piece even in a storage unit!

To most people, 38 special and 9mm is considered fun but not the real deal although can be deadly if fired from a close range, just the clicking sound of 9mm while cocking it, is enough to scare away an intruder but not enough to challenge the big guns that these thugs have even if you are a sharp shooter.

Tracing gun owners can be difficult and can be a pain or the authorities if the records are not accurate.

Those involved in the 'Thug life' kind of sales care less about keeping the records or names but the almighty dollar they get out of it For this reason the data is always off, this is why Steve says the officers need better gadgets! For him he makes it sound like they are just toys but as I know, ..Deadly! What we say around here is to be aware of your surroundings, Steve was right, the fight goes on! We support any kind of security detail that can help. Keep our business premises safe, so our guests would never have to worry about being un safe while they shop. Forster and Pete' were grateful to the Chief of police for working with the local community to help keep the environment safer.

This must have been the hardest press conference for both of them, they never wanted to be in the lime light but work in the background and focus more on business development but this was for a worthy cause!

14
Evening Out.

THAT EVENING AS we both signed out after grueling meeting with the boardroom members, officially known as the 'Winners team' plus, the work we had to do after the meeting, I thought Al' would be dead tired and just drive home but that was not the case!

He said something about having a drink at Megan's, his ex-girl-friend. Showing surprise on my face.. Just spitting it out, I thought you guys broke up!

I had to ask!

Yes we did, he answered in a lower voice and apparently you are coming with me.. Don't ask questions! And it's not what you think!

He said that as if scared about the whole situation.

Then what is it?

I still asked anyway even though he didn't want to be asked.

She said she wanted to talk to someone.

And in this case she picked you?

I interjected! I can't think of any serious issue they have discussed lately because he would have mentioned it, if she is some kind of per-son that does not change her mind easily as he had previously told me.

My guess at that time, was that the other guy dumped her or was it something serious? I thought.

Al' said her work at the bank made her extremely busy so he rarely saw her, so I guess he had to create time for her tonight.

Well, I think it's a risky Idea to go to an ex-girlfriend's house and have a drink unless she has something up her sleeve which she's not telling you and you never know what to expect, I said to him.

He tried to calm me down.. And told me the Idea of me going with him was to neutralize the tight atmosphere after she answers the door.. So don't panic!

Nevertheless, I was completely un easy about the visit.

I don't know if I should give her a hug or just say hi and move to the sofa..

Would that be a good Idea? He was thinking aloud.

A little agitated because my evening plans were ruined by this abrupt meeting between him and Megan. Man, you should have told me earlier, you have no Idea if I had plans this evening.. But anyway you are lucky and you can count on me to be there tonight just give me a heads up on what time and where we are meeting before we go there okay?

For the past months, we have had a lot of work to cover It was amazing to see him create the chip he had tried to identify and patent, this took a long time, he said finding correct software was crucial for his private interest which he took pride in.

A few times, I went to see him, sometimes I would find him talking to himself, if he saw me standing by the garage door, he totally ignored my presence!

This time, he was arguing loud.. If soft sounds of music has been known to reactivate a human brain, supposedly in a comatose stage then wireless massage beads could be a possible solution to stop blood clots and accelerate blood flow in elderly people that are prone to blood clots situations?

And by making wireless ear buds, those manufactures celebrated a great accomplishment to music lovers who were tired of constant entangling of the cords.. Detangling every time a phone call came through or just listening to music, detangling in time not to lose the call, you had to speed it up, right?

Yes! Quite a pain!

That's correct!

Well, good enough but why are we not researching aggressively for other possibilities?

That, I couldn't answer but I hope innovators are on it! I let him argue his case across, .. Or rather to his mind because he was not addressing me.. but talking to an empty space..

Pacing back and forth in his three car garage.. I thought his mind was full of constructive thoughts just waiting to be implemented!

His complicated lab was divided in two Sections, one section was completely fenced off using clear glass divisions in a rectangular two different shapes of microscopes sitting shape on one of the shelves.

The other remaining part of the garage had counter tops with gadgets on both tables, his car was parked under canvas shade outside the garage..

How long have you been standing there, he asked me at one point..

I don't know! It was just interesting listening to your thoughts, which was loud because I heard them, I replied!

But don't worry, I get those thoughts too.. sometimes especially when I can't solve a problem at hand! And yes! Research has created more discoveries than anybody would have thought in the twentieth century, think about Cancer treatments and more... my good gesture was to make him feel better about his puzzle sort of situation so to speak and only should make him feel like a genius who he really was, well thought Ideas, he just needed to make or see them come to life!

If this made him feel better, then good, if it did not,

I wasn't going to be surprised, he was hard to understand when it came to things like this!

Al' has been affected by his former colleague suffering with serious burn wounds and was in constant pain Al' thought as soon as he could fix the missing pieces of his work and complete the project, he could get answers to some unresolved matters which I assumed must had been in medical field.

It seemed like a new world opened right before him, seeing his excitement to continue with his research his research, he did not elaborate his intentions on the project he had in place but on the other hand, I did not dig deeper to find out the details of his research journal.

He quickly disappeared between the veneer cabinets, I will be right back, let me freshen up a little, He said as he climbed the stairs to the main house from his garage..

I will be here.. I shouted back!

Looking around but not touching a thing in his garage,

I wondered how much time he spent in that garage, everything in it looked so complicated!

As Al' walked back, he told me not to be late, he was winding up his project so he could meet me later for the mission at hand that evening!.

When we met later that evening, I could see that Al' was happy I agreed to go with him. let's hit the road, he said but not before picking up fresh flowers from a local vendor and it seemed like this vendor knew his taste, naming each branch by name. I was just standing there in silence..

Those are her favorites.. He said it in a way as if to redeem his doubtful mind against Megan !

Shaking my head.. I'm not saying anything, I couldn't blame him, they dated for a long time.

It was about twenty to thirty minutes-drive but with heavy traffic it was definitely the wrong time on the. interstate, it would take us double or more than the normal time, but I guess we had to just go and get it behind us at some point.

It seemed like forever for Al', I couldn't understand the anxiety, I thought he hated Megan for dumping him but as it turned out, he just wanted that day to be done and over with!

One stop light before we pull up at Megan's drive way..

I was rather surprised to see balloons tied to the door and my guess is OMG, we are crashing a baby shower!

But as it turned out, it was a surprise birthday party for Al', probably the last they'd share together having broken up, for some reason women have this forgiving heart!

I was thinking but did not mention it to Al' wow! Who would have thought?

Sweet surprise party of three, Al', me and Megan Talking to him previously, he told me marriage was not their first priority but friendship, he lost grip somewhere and the relationship fell apart!

what scared him the most was that, marriage was a long term contract and he wasn't ready for that commitment yet! It had to be really a trying situation and he is one guy that does not accept failures. In his mind, it wasn't just forth coming! He was not successful in spicing up their relationship, it just got a little boring, that's what he says happened!

I just thought, he was extra hard on himself, what he forgets is that nobody is perfect. In life all these things we do and succeed has passed some tests, there's got be some situation of failure at some point, a record to look through and do better next time.

Even though they had broken up for a while, Al' was surprised that Megan remembered his birthday he admits that he has a lot going on in his mind that his birthday would be the last thing he can think of!

We got a great reception at Megan's but he got a little mad when Megan brought about the past bitter sweet relationship issues. As the evening went by, he moved very freely in this house, made some desert, ice cream and strawberry fruit toppings..

What can I say?

Good for Al' to just get away for a while, he is such a workaholic, missing out on important things in life, so I thought. I only hope that this will be a start from where they left it!

Megan still remembers with a passion, the story her late grandmother told her to be careful and that all that glitters is not Gold!

Al' stood up!

Come on! Don't give me that attitude ? Calming him down, she asked him to sit down back on the couch.

Al', I have no one in my life, I was just watching my footsteps, treading carefully, okay? She said!

I know when I'm ready it's going to be great Al' ,

You were just two paces ahead of me, that's all!

You should know. I still care about you, she said candidly. Al' jaws dropped! Really?

Watching your steps while you break my heart? He said, somewhat in anger.

Well, if that's how you felt then I'm sorry!. She told him. but remember that you were reluctant at some point too.. So don't blame me entirely.. she told him.

Oh well, it's too late now..

Al' looking out to the backyard through the glass window.. Punching into the air still holding a clenched fist before relaxing up.. He did not say another word, Probably he was thinking of those precious moments they shared in that house!

Looking across the room with his back leaning on the closed window, in a startled moment to face Megan as if to say.. Now what? This sucks!

It was kind of crazy for me to think of a very strong guy looking vulnerable like this, one of those awkward moments Look Al' I'm truly sorry…

Reaching closer, Say no more.. Say no more, she hushed him putting her finger on his lips, she gave him a light kiss on the lips, I was doing that silent clap.. yes.. she did!

A daring woman, I thought!

He was still in a dazed moment but he did not turn his head away and my guess is, he enjoyed it! Hey, you want a little more wine? Looking at me trying to change the topic.. Sure! I replied! Watching every drop, I sipped my wine in silence, I felt embarrassed caught between the two of them. A few moments later, there was a knock at the door at this time, my mind is running wild, thinking it could be the new boyfriend coming home from work only to find the ex-boyfriend in the house, disastrous! I reached over to Al' and said to him, man if you want to leave, this is the time! Yes! He said it almost in a whisper..

Sorry I got you into all these!

Oh yeah? Well may be it was the only way she could get you to come here..

And now you know how She feels about you!

It's got to bite, I told him!

If she needed someone to talk to as you told me there is absolutely nothing wrong with her inviting the man she previously loved!

Yeah right! Previously, correctly said!

There's nothing between us now, Ok?

Al' said to me almost like spitting out the words!

Fine, fine.. Calming him down I reminded him that he was the one who invited me there.. I don't get it! Why did she have to break up with me, was she not sure of her actions?

I don't know ! Don't ask me that, I said...

I don't expect you to answer it either! He snapped walking a few paces back and forth...

Trying to think hard, I watched in silence and tried not to trigger anything! Anyway forget it! He said. This is just like those stories you always hear about that if you see someone special the next thing in your mind, you feel something... you think you really like them, you only hope they feel the same way too, but not likely...

So you think of a plan to get noticed! You could see it working so your mind tells you to go for it!

You break the ice! He said.

So you did not break the ice? I asked him.

No! I mean, I liked her at first sight but this was a long time ago during company's Expo, the company I worked for before this one sent me to be the representative and there she was, very polished, respectful and the smile? Wow! Striking!

That was then ... We finally met and the relationship was going great past two years until this one evening, she called me to tell me she had a second thought.. So I thought she met Someone else, may be better than me.

He said all these in almost a broken voice!

When she is done talking to who knows who? At the door, let's get the hell out of here..

Al' said to me in a low tone...

Yes! Deal! I said.

Megan was talking to some elderly man who preferred not to come inside the house or was he restrained by Megan?

I don't know that for a fact. Megan closed the door behind her and escorted the man to his car, you won't believe this but as she stepped away to the driveway, we both rushed to the window to see who he was or what was going on but to our surprise it was, just a simple goodbye and a firm hand shake. What? That's what Al' said in surprise! Man, he really had his doubts!

when she got back, we pretended we were deep in some interesting story.. She knew we were a little tensed, so she spoke openly to
address Al' but I heard it too..

Hey! I plan to sell this house and that was a prospective buyer...
We dropped the negative thought and just laughed it off! Okay, Al'
said to her and how come you have never mentioned this to me?

Well, I planned to tell you but I have been busy shopping for a new
place, and I also want you to arrange to move your classic ford from
my garage I can have it painted...

He knew she was going to say this but did not expect it today
That's news! He said. Okay, I will let you know tomorrow thanks for
today, seriously, I mean that! Al' confirmed to her, he will organize
towing services as soon as he could to get the car out.

Happy birthday Al', she told him..

With a lump in his voice.. He responded with gratitude, a hug
and a light kiss on her cheeks this time, Thank you! Megan, means a
lot he told her!

We really should be on our way, at this point, I said, I stood up
to leave and reached over to say goodnight to her I didn't care if she
knew me or not, as far as I was concerned, my job was done here!

I thanked her for the evening and walked through the door. I
left them to talk for a few more minutes. I saw that she was a very
reserved person. I could tell that she was tensed initially but later she
relaxed and offered us a glass of wine plus throwing Al' a birthday
party, It was the coolest thing ever !

On the driveway, Al' told me, he was almost certain, him and
Megan are not ready to get back together but was open to discussion
on other things that might interest them.

Mmh.. Interesting! I thought.

Al' described the evening as the best in the recent months, and I
couldn't agree more.. I just regretted having been there, this was his
moment Would things have been different if I wasn't there? Who knows!

Al' stopped to see me drive off first, then followed me until the
first stop light then we both went different ways. To sum it up, it was
some interesting evening!

15
Never losing it.

THIS MORNING THERE had been signs of windstorms and I'm glad I don't have to stay late like Yesterday, Al' didn't even look up but was busy going through some files on his desk while I was selecting what was to go to press and what we need for next week starting new season, I couldn't help but mention about last evening.

I told Al' how I was blown away, I did not know his ex-girlfriend could be such a sweet personality! I was waiting for his reaction, so I paused... For a moment, I thought he did not hear me but he suddenly looked up, I got his attention this time!

Don't say that! He snapped! You don't know her, his eyes wide open this time, she made me feel like, it wasn't me she was looking for, she didn't find the 'IT' in me so I wish the lucky guy well!

When I met Carla, I thought why not? I have been seeing her the past three weeks and so far, so good! He said smiling, as it was, only a man in a relationship with a nice girl knows what's in store for him, guess work doesn't work in this case! So I thought this was the best time to ask about his new companion.. I sat down before asking, so is she anyone I know?

Nope! He said with confidence..

Good luck, man! I just don't want you to get hurt again! All the same I know you can handle it! I told him. Don't worry, I'm taking it slow this time.

Thanks for your concern but for right now, I'm not into a serious relationship, just looking for good Company, may be later..

Alright man, whatever works for you! I commented.

And you know how busy I am, a lot of things in my mind.

I have a promotion next week and the forth coming shareholders events, not complaining, don't get me wrong, I love my job and I never want to lose it at this time of the year, got to stay focused and set a good example to the rest of the team by choice to which I had already made up my mind to be the best as I can be to reflect what the company expects of me.

It's just that it's hard to juggle all these stuff, keep a beautiful, demanding girlfriend and stay sane!

I hear you on that one, just keep your head up! I told him. Look, we shared a drink with Carla one evening and we just hit it off!

I realized she is more country than I thought and I love that about her! He revealed to me., he even mentioned that he plans to spend his vacation in the west and if Carla was interested in going with him, she was more than welcome, she could have the prestige of riding horses with him at his uncle's ranch in Flagstaff Arizona.

Shaking his head smiling, he said she does not believe in the short form of his name, He laughed about it!

Go for it! I told him. And by the way, how old is your young beauty?

Al' looked at me in surprise, ladies don't tell their age so don't ask!

Easy man, easy.. I did not mean to stir anything, just a question! You could be tripping man, if she is way too young, she will sure break your heart! Just me thinking! That's okay, he waved his hand to me, flipping through his files ..Anyway once again, thanks for accompanying me to Megan's place yesterday.

You are welcome! I told him. And just to add to what you already found out, ladies like to cuddle, they'd like the assurance that the relationship is secure, if they don't feel it, the break up is imminent!

Al' did not say a thing still engrossed in his work which I do respect him for doing what he preaches.

Time to complete my work as well, I had to confirm certain prices with Josh, so I quietly closed Al's door not to distract him from his work.

Meanwhile at the sales floor as I approached to talk to Josh as always Gerald was there cracking a joke with a clerk, this was his first stop from his job at the state local park. He was always loud knowing who he was after meeting him several times at the local Pub.

I knew he was now a happy man at least after a long term therapy.

His life story consisted of very sad situations but I could see he was finally getting over it!

In Vietnam during his time, he got involved with a beautiful girl that later became his wife.

He was not allowed to bring with him his wife to the country.

On his way back to the US, he got into a huge confrontation with the cultural leaders, he still plays the scene clearly in his head as if it was more like a movie scene but as it was for real a dramatic capture than anything he had ever seen in his life!

Tearing her off his arms was heart breaking!

Her late father was deeply involved with tribal commitments which included respect and maintaining their country's culture to book.

His daughter being involved with Gerald was considered disrespectful. Gerald was beaten, rolled over to the river edge inside a canvas sack and left for dead, he lost the battle and decided to return back to the US alone without his sweetheart, kind of sad!

Well, that was some unfortunate situation that can happen, to anyone during that era, he tried to console himself! The war was over but according to him it wasn't!

A call of duty? You could only expect a job well done, the next plan was to get back home and have this great life as he explains it which he had envisioned for years but that was not the case!

He carries her passport size photo in his wallet, he simply does not trust his cell phone gallery, you lose these phones or they break... He says, and I don't trust storing anything in the cloud, a web designed to store photos or files you don't necessarily need or use frequently but tell you what I'm old school, I do things the way I feel or comfortable and feel safe with because all these new technology people are so engrossed in, anyone can access those files and use them for the wrong reasons, he was telling a fellow patron seated next to him!

He shows her picture off every time he meets a new friend at the pub where Frankie, the bar tender probably was the most loyal friend he could tell almost anything so long as he was still willing to lend his ear to listen to many other war stories!

Frankie was in his twenties, he had no freaking idea of what Vietnam war was like, he could only imagine the scenes from the movies he watched as a kid growing up Saving his lunch money just to buy pop corns that tasted so good, he remembers those people at the lobby, or behind that all glass counter were generous with the butter part of it!

Weekends were relatively busy but I could see the two friends gave each other a thumbs up when something was funny or if he needed a refill.

Gerald would show Milne's picture, to friends, beautiful girl huh? Isn't she? He would ask any sympathetic friend, his friends would answer in the affirmative, simply because she was really beautiful or the other reason could be because they did not want to hurt his feelings more than he had already been hurt, he remembers her fondly...

He was extremely saddened by her death, he found out six months after her death simply because the family kept it under wraps, to be exact it was eight years after he left that country, his friends who thought he deserved to know about her death delivered the sad message... Never the less, he took it as a grown man, painful but hey what you 'gonna do' Huh? He asks! Life goes on, the living have to live! Life is a bitch! As he describes it. Gerald was a lonely man, his drinking buddies were left at the bar, he only got to see them when he got back there.

Rosalinda was one of them, she worked at a small convenience store and at sixty five she showed no signs of ever slowing down, the gas station was the busiest, built right after a major intersection no doubt, she met good and respectful customers, the regular ones who knew her by name or the ' hang over droopy' faces but she knew how to handle them all.

Motherly love is what they all need, she says.

I finished my assignment for the day and dropped of the prints to Al's office, to my surprise he had not left yet he looked up and asked what I was doing during the holiday weekend. Just going to the range with daughter, got to teach the girl everything I know in regards to self Defense and how to operate a simple nine mil.

You? I asked him... Oh I've got to tow that car out of Megan's garage and make room at my place..

Mm, I guess you will be busy then, have a good weekend. Thanks you too! He said as I was on my way out of his office. I couldn't forget to congratulate Jim, one of the techs, just became a grandpa two days ago.

Hey ! How are you? Grand pa' right? Yes! I feel blessed, never been better...

He was truly happy..

I'm happy for you man... I told him

Have you seen the baby yet? I asked him,

Oh yeah!

my son called me as Katie, his wife went into labor, best news! She tried every fertility treatment she could get but nothing happened ! Thanks to the genius doctor that came up with a better plan for them and with the latest technology available they were able to conceive. I could see that he was truly appreciative of the doctor that helped his kids! .

I'm happy for them, I am just a little worried for my son, him being in the middle class, you know how inflation has caught up with majority of hard working Americans, I hope things get better in this country, he said!

It's everyone's hope, I told him.

Going fishing some day! Huh? That's in the plan in the near future.. He replied with a smile,. Well, have a good one.. I told him, I had to wish him well, never ruining a good moment! At least he deserved to be happy !

16
Improving outlook.

AL' WAS ALMOST done with his paper work, he showed me the list of certain values that needed to be discussed at the boardroom, mainly at the check outs.

1. How to better manage transactions,
2. How do managers concerned track and keep the sales records
3. The necessity of hiring courtesy clerks
4. Better communication skills.
5. Required gadgets and coin change dispensers.
6. How to make shopping experience even better.

Why the last one? I mean people are moving away from everything plastic but towards digital.

He said is it because people don't use cash much these years? I asked.

Don't get me wrong, It's still acceptable form of tender even if the guest decides to use coins.. Al' tried to put that in my mind..

Oh well I agree..

The boardroom was heated up with a ton of questions from Staying current with all forms of payments to changes on how to handle traveler's checks and how to make the systems work better plus what was to be implemented immediately.

Oh yes, I remember situations when outdated systems couldn't work, lines were extremely long at check outs!

I told him. It is not just the norm, there's got to be a better way and we are changing it all to make shopping fun and pleasant to every one of our guests!

Can you imagine the truth is, at the moment it's a lot quicker to get a cup of coffee at the local coffee shop just with your I phone, he quipped! ..

No coins accepted at the coffee shop? I asked..

Of course it's not like that! He defended his statement, We both laughed at the comment! Every form of payments as regulated by the law of the land is acceptable, it's just that less and less people use cash...just like You don't want to be held longer than you expect at the drive through because someone was still counting pennies, you don't want to be that guy everyone is honking at, right?

Al' asked me, he knew the answer to that question so I didn't bother to answer.

Hey, that person just wants a fresh cup of coffee in the morning to start his day!

Later that day, I had to break a sweat, this was a team of winners, no pointing fingers, no matter what you do, own it because the main goal is what we accomplish for the company..

That's right ! It has always been on my mind! It was busy that day, time went by so fast. I was glad I met my goals for the day. Walking past the usual shade, we sat at break time, I saw the usual employees seated out relaxing but sometimes sensitive to certain opinions but a compliment, Yes sir!

Many times when I'm seated at the bench, It was hard to tell what Nicole would ask! Generally she would always ask questions about any new information from the board meetings but this time, I figured the catwalk was for some good reason.. I saw this coming as she approached!   How do I look? Her friend who was also a cashier like her had a wide grin...

You look great Nicole, what's shaking?

I asked! Just working on my looks! That's great, it's okay to feel good about yourself but the best thing is not to rely so much on what others have to say about you but rather believe in yourself!

If you are dieting for health reasons, that's okay but remember, do it for yourself but should not be for someone else! You should wake up every day feeling good about yourself no matter what size you are, you are God's best creation beautifully and wonderfully made!

So with that words of wisdom, take a step, have faith in yourself, you will sure feel great! I told her.

Aww.. Thank you! I will sure do that! She said as she walked away. Her friends were happy for her, she really looked great. As I popped my can of soda, I saw Claire approach, she is one of the longest serving cashiers break time? I asked her..

Of course! That's when I get to leave my station.. Her hoarse voice made her sound like she had smoked all her adult life, I could be wrong too. I'm almost going back to work but tell me, what was wrong with that guest who pulled you aside a few minutes ago? I asked.

Nothing serious, he was just some snoopy guest asking stupid questions.. She said smiling as if not to offend Really? I asked Yeah!

He was asking questions like why is the parking lot almost empty on a holiday like today, things like that, what I'm I supposed to say? So what did you tell him? I told him most customers are scared of traffic jams during holidays, cyber business is booming too which we have up and running website, so they either shop online and have the items shipped to them and besides, we have Self Checks outs and quick lanes, this saves time and creates a parking spot for the next guest, he had nothing more to say..

That was great Claire, that's my kind of girl! I told her, she was all smiles. If he was a competitor snooping, which I wouldn't be surprised, he picked the wrong girl.

Claire was the kind of person that would not entertain negative comments, that is how she was, staying positive at all times! Thank you Claire, This made her feel appreciated..

Oh yes! That's right! Give credit where it's worth! As I was leaving, I saw her pace through a magazine she had in her hands and I thought, bright people always have something to read, may be a lot of downloading and uploading in the works! I thought!

17
Getting Quorum.

HIRING QUALIFIED PERSONNEL to handle advertising matters was crucial because media approach was a big thing.

A lot of concerns on what image was Portrayed out there. If you are in a long term business, you never give your competitor the reason to bring you down, so it was important we discussed this on the next Boardroom, Bob had told me about it earlier in the day, he was trying to get as many members to attend.

I approached Bob to ask him all about the other details, holding files in his bosom and a pencil between his teeth, he tried to talk to me but one of the files fell off from his grip, kind of an awkward situation! I also saw that he had scribbled some notes including Insurance and I wondered if he was an Insurance producer himself.

Hey what are you doing at the moment? He asked me...

I told him, I was actually trying to locate him.

We talked for a little while, he mentioned about Insurance consultants coming to talk to the staff but before they do that, we will have some time to review what they've got especially when every board member should be present during Today's meeting.

Do they represent some insurance firm? I asked.. No! Bob said. They are actually an independent body, all these people coming have state licenses to operate here and of cause they both have a great experience having worked for different Insurance companies themselves. Each state has certain laws totally different from others so we need to get a clear cut information from these experts, he told me

Thinking to myself, I certainly want to put some money into annuity and would like to know more about the programs that can work better for me, may be increase my 401k contributions..

Who knows! I could use free and useful information anytime..

Okay, so please attend. Bob said to me.

Sure! I replied. I certainly didn't want to stay employed until I'm too old to do any practical work for myself. My dream is to retire when I'm still strong enough with a little bit of some money set aside, globe trot and just see the side I have not been able to see on short and programmed vacations!

And lastly, enjoy life as if it was my last day, get to smell a few roses… Mmh! I will be just fine..

I was deep in these thoughts that I did not hear Al's footsteps as he approached.. You must be thinking of something serious, is that right? He asked me.

A little, why? I asked.

Because I asked if you are attending the Tuesday's meeting and I did not hear response!

Well, that's right,, I'm thinking ahead of time, it's your slogan, remember? I said! You got me there! He just smiled. Here you go! He handed me the names of those he had listed to attend the meeting. I see my name on the top, why is this some kind of a hidden agenda? I asked

Of course not!

I just want you to attend and besides, You are a better communicator too, talk to the rest and make them understand the need to attend the meeting, there are a few changes on health products, after attending and understand your medical plans, you can make necessary adjustments, just know the right steps to take.

He turned around and left!

And boy did I have a lot to do!

It was time for me to complete my tasks for the day and present reports to the board before the end of the day!

18
Insurance Consultants.

THE BOARDROOM STARTED with the same classical music sound, low sounds of drum beats. Soft synthesizers... The jingle lasted for about two minutes to be precise!

This was Pete's Idea, to create a different atmosphere and release the tension from the nerves before discussing tough issues his love for music is great and he wished to display it anywhere he went This was already a state of the art boardroom, the music was just to compliment it!

That was what he believed in, he also wanted to create an atmosphere where all the managers can solve issues quietly without interference.

Andre' stood up to introduce the Insurance consultants to all the members of the boardroom. He also introduced us before he sat down. The first consultant moved to the center to access the microphone fixed to a podium. He mentioned that we all need a heads up to know how to choose right, what to do when making adjustments and which investment that befits your age, 'free look' period limit and how long one can wait before asking for cash surrender value, in case of a financial need.

Johnson, explained the difference in a couple of acts incorporated in insurance laws and acts.

options for certain for age preferred. He went on to say that it's important to read the contract because the document written between the insured and the insurer is binding to both parties.

The policy is effective by first premium being approved and the policy delivered to the insured. After the first premium, if anything happens to the insured, he or she who is insured or beneficiary will receive the same privilege but the truth of the matter is that the Insurance companies want the insured to stay alive to continue Paying premiums! Laughs in the boardroom... I thought isn't that the truth?

Moving on... Federal law allows terminated employee to stay in the group COBRA, which is simply Consolidated omnibus reconciliation Act, usually printed on booklet When you get hired, not a lot of details but you need to know that With market place' you could get less expensive options should you need to or moving out of the network.

You can also make none deductible contributions to ROTH IRA (Individual Retirement account) limits up to specified limits by choosing 403 B TSA.

On payroll deductions, your insurance agent should tell on the limits and remember accelerated benefits are paid. When insured is still living so the choice is yours employer's contributions to a qualified plan earn tax deferred interest which benefits employee.

Employees receive certificate of coverage but not the policy.

Bob stood up, to ask questions about terminally ill Patients. Johnson said that most insurance companies don't want to deal with that, more often than not, they would sell the Policy to an investor in a VIATICAL settlement This may not sound like a good deal but can be beneficial to the already ill insured where the coverage may continue 'as is' to keep the policy active and does not require further medical examination.

It is unlawful for an insurance producer replace a policy to another or try to push the insured to buy a product they don't need.

How about seniors? How can they tell the best coverage to get especially medical?

Bob asked... He had his father in a retirement home, medical bills are endless. So Johnson explained further to him what basic coverage means. Basic coverage through Medi-Gap:- From Plans, A,J,K, and L Plan 'A' will give the patient just the basic benefits 'D' will cover skilled nursing and foreign travel emergency and at home recovery.

Medi-Gap plan 'J' will cover basic benefits, Skilled nursing Facility co-Insurance, foreign travel Emergency and preventative care.

Plan 'K' includes basic benefits, skilled Nursing facility, co-Insurance 50% medi-care. Part 'A' deductible 50% Medi-Gap, plan 'K' will cover benefits and skilled nursing facility and up to 75% . changes to Any of these can only be approved by Insurances director, otherwise the policy remains the same.

The main reason to insure or add a rider on existing policy for a child is to provide the child with benefits in the event that the parents die before the child becomes an adult. That coverage is called Level Term life. If there's more than one child and a parent wishes not to name them, individually, the parent can simply state on the policy 'all My children' by class.

How about annuities? Another board member asked.

So he went on to explain that, most people buy annuities to earn tax deferred income to supplement retirement. In a none forfeiture provision, insured party can take a cash surrender on deferred annuity during the accumulation period a little different from social security which the contributor must have contributed in the amount of forty quarters to qualify for any payment. After he was done with the answers, Andre' stood up to thank the Insurance consultants for the information which was certainly needed. He kept standing as a gesture to show it was time to end the consultant's meeting.

I know you have a ton of questions but that's all for today, please get contacts and call them if you have further questions, he said winding up the meeting.

Alright! He exchanged strong hand shake with every one of them before they left. Without extensive explanation it's hard for People who are desperate to get insurance or to understand that it's not that simple but because they are probably running out of time and they don't have time to read those long documents written in small prints, they would simply pick What the agent suggested. Hey folks, always remember to read the documents you are trusting your health with.

He said before making his exit.

19
Entrepreneurship

ANDRE' AND JOSH had just completed working on the new LCD 'touch and find' screens to help guests with the company Applications. Although the system had been acting up lately but hoped the data reboot system they applied would enhance guest experience.

This was probably going to be Andre's last assignment, taking an early retirement, he was going to need some time to sum up his plans. Andre' had gotten attached to some of the staff members who started off with him and he wanted them to have a better life even after leaving current job, so his final gift of knowledge.

He decided to invite business consultants to give them some heads up!

Sanders, worked for a consolidating company, He explained what his company managed to do within his community and banks that were willing to cover the Programs initiated within his group.

He explained how to avoid credit card charges because failing to make just one payment is enough for them to report your name to the credit report bureau which is damaging. Anytime you get to apply for financial assistance, just know they will look you up! You don't want to be the bad ca se, because signs of financial struggle only means a red flag to financial institutions One step to financial freedom is having savings of some Sort, staying longer in debt ruins your credibility to almost anything that requires finances including getting hired in a financial institution or a job requiring employee to handle cash.

The company interviewing for the open positions will never mention this as to why they never called. Reason? The hiring committee decided against it and fears the new hire could be a threat to the business. There's credit card programs that can consolidate two or three credit card debts and this can give some relief. School, medical bills, premiums and any other business, all these can sink anyone in deep debt.

What they do is freeze the cards and pay the debt in full, then have only one account to pay through their credit card relief plan until your financial status changes, this can help stop falling into the same trap again that brought about the debts!

Sanders started on a humble beginning but got his big break after buying tax sale homes, the next was easy, as he phrased it, he said the a foreclosed homes was a major stepping stool, he made a deal with the home owner paid it off remodeled it, sold it at a profit and he never stopped investing ever since his first sealed deal.

The best trick, keep account active and running.

Banks will be glad you asked for a loan especially if you have been a customer for a while and beginning even at least six months because they make money when the customer pays the charges and they'd rather keep this business with them than if the customer went to their competitor.

Hey, about credit card debts, I was one of those that spent lavishly, I learnt my lesson and I have never looked back.

Mmm... Drinking a glass of water.. And swallowing it with a sound to it taking a moment with a gesture to show what the topic meant to him!

Yes, I mean that! Chocking in credit card debt my only way out was to get help and I did! My real Estate business is currently represented in twenty States and counting. Anybody can do this!

Anybody interested can check the counties that you have interest on for public records, local government offices and most advertisements are displayed either at the door or at the gates of the foreclosed home.

The next thing to do is take a drive and confirm if the information on the realtor's site is genuine being scammed can be devastating but once you've made up your mind, work the price like a professional, remodel and increase the value and put it back on the market, this could be a stepping stone to upgrade into buying a million dollar Homes and upgrade from there.

It starts to look like a movie and you have the power to pick your characters, starring you!

How does that sound? He asked those in attendance!

Pretty good! They replied!

So learn the tricks of the trade and strike the deal when the price is right. Expertise gets into place with progress but I can tell you, mine came after Some mistakes that I made, he said!

Selling too early when I could have been a little patient and would have sold the house for fifty grand more, I guess we all learn from our mistakes, you don't have to go through that if you plan well. Avoid balloon type of loans but go for fixed rates. Remember to keep colors neutral, furnish it to help boost and quicken the sale. Love what you do and never give up trying!

Next to give a speech was the beautiful Alison, she was feeling it and she proved it!

Moving on to the podium she mentioned about persistence and performance and good results just like, Sanders had explained earlier, that don't give up on your dreams. She went on to explain that most consumers go by brand names after seeing results or quality so whatever you invest in, consider two things keeping a good business name, trend and keep quality products, Or depending on area of interest make quick money and get out!

Big entrepreneurship doesn't come easy, just like Fashion designers, pretty smart too..

Fashion houses:-

They organize fashion parades and bring fresh faces of new models to catch the attention of old and new customers..

It might not be surprising to see that during the fashion week, their websites will be showing what they plan to show case on runway but has not been seen yet but can be discounted if your order is more than one piece!

Smart move? Absolutely!

By attending or watching the fashion week, the consumer's mind will be triggered right away to order it, a small caption will explain the selection is limited, then there will be a rush to get what you like, the anxiety in mind of a consumer gets greater, thinking of product availability! In most cases, consumers will still order anyway much to the delight of the sales representatives!. The main reason is to make it look like if you don't order now then you might not get what is on the runway and by the end of the show the fashion moguls are laughing all the way to the bank because they created the demand, then made the products available and made huge sales!

Some of the boardroom members were obsessed with designer labels..

And that discussion was quite welcome!

Finally, someone with the right skills, and some savings kept a side and proper guidance, you sure can succeed, she completed her speech! At the end of all discussions, the consultants contacts were displayed on the screen so any member interested in following up with them can do so.

20
Andres' Last Boardroom.

AFTER ALL THE board members sat down, Andre' stood up and addressed the members, reminding them how the boardroom started and what they have achieved within the years. It's a milestone!

This is a state of the art Boardroom where you can access whatever you need to improve the business, from organizing workshops to conference calls, privacy and anything you could do globally and updated and modern presentation and new gadgets to go with it!

We have done great folks, it's time for me to move on, Andre' said with a passionate voice.... I have had very supportive assistants, including everyone in this room, you have worked hard to see the success we have today.

The room was silent!

My successor as you all know has a great track record in retail and previously a business consultant. I can assure you with that kind of experience, he can step into my shoes without a problem..

The members clapped..

He paused for a moment to allow the clapping to subside, when the clapping stopped he proceeded.

Andre' explained more on how to make things work without straining. He also talked about being wise when making judgments!

Myles was very attentive as Andre' explained certain issues Andre' in this case was addressing Myles, you can be assured, you are taking over from me a very organized team that is geared for success only. If you work with them, you will achieve a lot!

Projecting that information to us he called out, hey I know Myles will work with you on the same page, knowing what the winners team is all about! Myles nodding his head in agreement and waved to the rest of the board members to confirm what they have just heard!

Cheers! Hand clapping... We all knew what Andre' meant. Look here folks, I'm no superman, you can do the same things that I did to make things work and uplift this business. I had to do what is right at all times because I knew the fruits will be achieved some day and more so, my faith in God and here we are today. No regrets!

And for you ? Pointing across the room, you have to keep going on! He told members of the boardroom!

Andre' was honored in many categories for his outstanding commitment to his work, never at any time did he boss over employees but worked with them as a team. Apparently his style made working environment adaptable, employees will miss him. The Boardroom was his brain child!

The Boardroom closed for the day but not without Andre' getting big hugs and best wishes from everyone.

Jim moved forward to give Andre' a hug..

Oh Andre' we will miss you! Jim told him I was just doing my job, Andre told him, You did a tremendous job! I will keep you in prayers and you have done better than most and to that is a big encouragement!

Jim loved to read from the scriptures, his lifestyle had been more about his faith. I'm pretty sure he likes to hear more about faith matters so what Andre' had said earlier revived his spirit! In his car, he sat quietly, with a small but bright light which he straps around his head to enable him to read his Bible.

This was kind of the norm for him, whenever his wife had to work late, he would sit in his car and read his favorite book while waiting for her. His wife worked at the same mall location late shift.

As I passed near his car one night, Jim was talking to Bob who apparently was an atheist. I could see his balding head from the shining lights around the parking lot. You've got to peruse this book, every leaf has some kind of wisdom related to it! It's believers encyclopedia, Sizing himself on his car seat, It's something he liked to do when expressing himself!

He was still talking to Bob who parked his car next to his car.

Give me a break!

Bob was not pleased with what Jim just said!

What did you say, Encyclopedia?

Bob asked angrily!

Yes to me it is! Jim replied. You don't get it, do you? Never mind, I did not expect you to understand Anyway..

Jim said to him.

It looks like Bob was not done yet.. You believers think you know everything and others know nothing! Is that what you are saying? Bob blurted out!

No! No! That's not what I meant.. You have to read it a couple of times to understand it!

I have no intentions of reading it and besides I believe in being a good person and doing good, may be some day be rewarded in some way but what I don't want is being locked in some brain washing religious belief!

You know since you have no intention of reading the Bible, the word of God is dead to you and you have no way of knowing the truth! Jim replied, and for your information only those in Some kind of cult faith can get brain washed.... But I'm not! He waved his hands in some practical gesture as he said it.. If I offended you then I'm sorry but I'm not sorry about my faith, Jim told Bob.

No, that's fine good night Jim! Bob shouted as he rolled up his windows and raved his car off the parking lot..

I heard this argument halfway as I was talking on the phone and besides, I had a very long day, I did not want to get involved but I knew it!

Nobody messes up with his faith! Take it easy man! I told him as I passed closer to his car, his windows were rolled down so I knew he heard me although I didn't expect him to respond but he just nodded, that was good enough at least he did not ignore a good gesture...

He was backing out of the curb at the time and slowly moved closer to the front part of the parking lot where his wife would notice the car quickly when she comes out of work, freshly new grandparents, they had a lot to Celebrate.

As I sat in my car, relieved that the day was over. I took a minute to review all that had happened during the day, kept my folders inside my work briefcase and left for the night.

21
Farewell Party.

THINGS WERE ALREADY a buzz at the club house, Andre' was member at this club so we were not about being timed out, it was a little bit out of town but Was befitting for this occasion.

It was almost five days since Andre' announced his departure, things were already abuzz, the phones couldn't quit ringing, lots of inquiries, I promised to help Josh find correct remote gadgets for public address System within the hour.

Friends and guests who knew about Andre' leaving kept the phone lines busy the whole day. We got the preparations out of the way and we were ready for the function. Things moved so fast but Al' was sure he got everything under control. Brenda, Marisa and the other ladies offered to create their own designs without the help of a florist..

For real, they decked the tables elegantly never too much and not less, just right!

Friends and employees brought a bunch of gifts.

I saw a lot of cards and teddy bears placed on top often he lined up tables set aside for gifts.. from us, we bought him a set of new golf clubs, still Art and some collectable miniature classic Cars.

Some of the people that brought gifts included guests that considered him as a brother in the neighborhood If they needed a product, he would go out of his way to find it and ship it or call the guest to come Collect it..

They loved that! He understood their interests perfectly well! The kids at a local school nearby also brought tones tons of Teddy bears, okay may be not tons but more than we expected!

As for Pete and Forster, let me just say, they gave him a great send off!

No doubt in my mind, he was amazed at the love, he received from everyone, you never know these things, what people think about you until you see it, actions speak louder than words, I thought!

Andre was a simple man, he did not like anything exaggerated about him, he still insisted, he was just doing his job, same thing he would expect anybody in this type of business to do.

His smile remained halfway to the corner of his mouth, as he thanked everyone that showed up at his farewell party and all the friends that brought him gifts, he said he was grateful.

His family sat close to him, Andre's speech was short, forthright and encouraging.

Bob's emotional speech described Andre' as a great motivator, which he really was. And everyone that was paying attention and was not intoxicated yet clapped their hands and cheered!

Al' was now the official spokesperson, he also gave a vote of thanks to everyone that attended the farewell party and didn't forget to mention a few things about Andre', he cracked a joke and everyone busted laughing! He tapped his glass and asked us to toast to Andre' he cheered, to Andre'! In unison they said and took a sip of their champagne! Nice! I thought!

I could hear the cling, cling sound coming from the champagne glasses, even though my team was sad but at the same time happy For Andre'. Whatever he decided to do with his life after this was up to him! Al' was not done, holding his glass still high up at the time, I knew he had something more to say.

Hey! Everyone, Al' asked, what do we believe in?

Success! They roared back, I mean those who were paying attention, most were excited to share the comment. And if we fail? He continued. Pick up and move on, We never give up trying! They thundered back.. Go! go! That's the winners team, you can't stop them! By the way those were Andre's favorite words that's why Al' said them!

Myles gave an assuring speech to confirm that he would do what it takes to keep the performance upbeat, he thanked Andre' and wished him well in his new endeavors!

Andre' made his way to the barbeque table, he took a chip and made a dip at the salsa Dish " guacamole' dishes- spiced mashed avocado mixed with freshly diced tomatoes, onions, Serrano pepper, a pinch of salt, lime juice and finely chopped cilantro.

The next table had several Sake drinks, natural flavors, sushi chef waited but he just looked at the packaging of the drinks Andre' complimented the chef but didn't eat from that plate.

There was also freshly cut celery in a 'bloody Mary' which lots of people like to mix chili pepper sauce, One (tot) or a shot of vodka, lime juice a pinch of salt and water.. Tempting!

Andre' looked at it and skipped it but picked a leaf of Lettuce, he also ate some pieces of chopped roasted cucumber and snack on it as he walked around the buffet table. There was a salad bar and lots of fruits arrangements.

Andre' was chatting and mixing with guests and employees in attendance at the club. He took snap shots with them before leaving the event.

The evening was spent well.

Al' and I had to leave to go to our favorite pub where Carla was waiting for Al' so he had to excuse himself never the less, the party wasn't going to end soon.

As for guests who stayed behind to enjoy the spoils, it was upon them to decide on how late they wanted to party. Thinking about it, what was left for us, It was time to climb the ladder, I don't care what others say but I want to see myself at the top someday soon because as for me, the sky is the limit!

After that weekend party, I could almost guess what most employees preferred to be included on the menu, and that was... free beers!

The next day after partying, things had to go on, it was business as usual.

Myself and Al' had to work early I was rather surprised Al' was not at his office, I hope everything went fine with Carla last night and he didn't get into some kind of fight! Lately he had become more protective over Carla. I tried calling him but it went straight to his voicemail.

Hey man, get your ass here, so we can finish the project!

I kept on recording the message, you are already one hour late..

It was one of these phone services that allowed you to listen to your message before sending it or confirm it, when I listened back, I thought my message was a little mean.. so I erased it and re-recorded a new one which I told him to call me as 'ASAP' Short form of as soon as possible!

mmh, things might have been good With Carla, I thought When Al' finally showed up looking ragged and just out of it! You look terrible! You didn't sleep at all? I asked?

A little, he replied.. Okay I understand! I said to him.. No, you don't! He said, looking away at this time. My mind was racing at this time, could it be that bad? Carla being ten years younger than him ?

may be a lot of activities Until late into the night. I didn't tell him this thought, but it turned Out to be close, he accepted that him and Carla went a little crazy, that night, Carla calls it the carpet lounge!

Some, alone time just the two of them sitting down on the carpet leaning on some large floor cushion in front of a fire place, a chilled glass of wine in hands, just a perfect evening!

He said that with a lot of excitement!

Then came kitchen counter top, don't tell me you haven't tried this one, with the sound of water running down the sink and someone decides to get wet, No?

He asked me but he knew he wasn't going to get an answer from me so, I just shook my head and said, not yet!

Al' going on with his story, he said after their wet experience at the kitchen sink, they moved to the bathroom where he told her to keep her hands on the sink handles because she was being distractive as he was trying to brush her hair down at her request because she thought it was romantic..

whatever happened after that, he couldn't remember .. He felt the snap sound coming from his back, he must have sprained his back... That was his thought, his lower spine area felt like some bone was sticking out, it was as painful as hell!

He said the pain lasted for the rest of the night, she tried all the magic, to make him feel better but nothing! I should have known better, he chuckled!

He said, he had to go to the Emergency Room early morning. With a little touch, stretch out exercise, a wooden roll bar on his back, shock buttons and a massage made a big difference! He later admitted that Sex was a little different with her but it was fun!

He felt more fulfilled as he explained it!

It was really nice to have those feelings again, he mumbled. smiling ...

whatever happened! It was just bad luck! You know she is hot, I couldn't resist! On a light note, I told him to take it slow next time!

I'm happy for you! I told him.

Carla is the only girl I have heard call him by his full name Alejandro and he never complained or made that angry look.. He often complained that the name was too long..

And we made fun of him to blame it on the priest who suggested that name to his mom!

Not funny, guys.. Stop it! He would say.. To her, that was his name and there was nothing wrong with saying it, If he had a bad childhood where bullies made fun of his name, that was his problem, but should not be important, he would snap at us! Al' would have been happy if she didn't mention it, but all he could say to her anytime she called his full name was.. Okay, Bombshell, whatever you say! Sure, we can turn into some jelly, mostly around the knees! He joked!

We just laughed and went inside to Start our project where Myles was waiting to go through some files with him. Al' will have to take it easy until his back gets better... and if lucky, he has to avoid Carla for the next couple of days..Or rather if he did, absolutely zero activities.

22
Myles steps it up.

IT'S BEEN TWO weeks since Andre' left, Myles was talking about creating impulse sales and so on. Walking through the sales floor, getting one on one conversation with department managers, getting to know them better, project plan for the day and their concerns.

He also reminded them to consider checking guests concerns by using their I pads in the early hours of the day to help them adjust better and meet the online demands.

That week marked the first boardroom Myles chaired after Andre' left, he had a lot to catch up on the boardroom minutes. It was also the time all managers on duty reviewed sales and the stock in place or any other business that raised concerns If not in physical attendance, no problem, any manager assigned at another location at that time could connect and attend via live broadcast.

The company provided accessories to enable every manager on duty to work efficiently. That was kind of cool...

I thought!

I would say that was an investment done right!

Good example, Brenda who could not attend, she was out with the girls to a book club but was able to attend turning on her phone into live broadcast mode, thanks to the latest technology, systems Work better with very little effort.

All these was Andre's Ideas, he believed that work was a lot better if we communicated better with each other at all levels..Strictly business and make it work, he emphasized! This was crucial, smooth and good communications! I thought this one anybody could relate to.

While, Brenda was waiting eagerly for the meeting to start, she would be happy to get back to her book club! Alright, everyone is here, ladies and gentlemen, let's get started.

Myles moved to the center of the room to full view of the rest of the members including those joining via live broadcast like Brenda.

Look guys, I don't expect you to turn yourselves into robots but we must aim at giving that a hundred percent service, raising a standard is very important and it will remain our goal! Myles said.

I expect you to perform your job and give reports however, what you can't handle let us discuss it and find ways of solving it right here in this boardroom.

So, you should know that your suggestions matter, we are open to discussions, we would also consider new options that work and no doubt, there's still a lot to be done! Since, I'm still working on many files Andre' had marked as important, but I will keep today's meeting short, let's work on immediate cases that needs to be addressed.

Members took turns in presenting their lists and gave recommendations on what they felt should be done.

Myles, promised to work with the team to enjoy a continued success.

To beat the odds, we must continue doing what we do in this region and to the rest of the world... Myles said I guess this was meant to tell anyone in doubts to start believing in him because of the fact that he was now the head of the team.

The meeting proved longer than Brenda expected, the big screen expressed her un easiness, it was that clear.

we could see it!

Expressions speaks volumes!

she was blinking more than usual, perhaps the weather was unfavorable from that open area she sat at the food court she and her friends were meeting for a meal, but she Stayed until the end of the boardroom meeting.

As Myles wrapped up the meeting, Brenda picked up her files...

good job everyone! She said, bye guys, extending her hands she blew the members some flying kisses before the screen Was shut off..

That was Brenda, bold but so un-datable... She thought all the men she met didn't measure up to her standards! At this point I could hear everyone's files flipping and comparing notes from page to page just quiet ..

I looked at the faces of the other managers I could tell that they were not fully convinced, Myles should not have closed the meeting without saying anything about some important issues they just presented him during the meeting.

Oh well .. Let's give him time, right now let's get down to some work.

Alright! Al' said. He walked across the room in an attempt to neutralize the mixed feelings within members., at this point no member spoke back to Al', he drank his coffee and chuckled a little, seeing that everyone was caught up between thoughts of whether Myles was a good communicator or was he just good at giving orders!

The question was, would he keep the same tempo when it comes to serious competition adjustments!

Al' cleared his throat to get attention, in case you are trying to compare the two men, you are wrong! Not everyone is the same nor are they the same in executing matters.. But each and every manager deserves to be given a chance to try new positions and so does Myles!

Al' was looking across one section of the room as if he expected some kind of answer or support from Bob and Josh.. Bob complied, he wanted to make it easy on Al' as they saw, he was getting frustrated ..

So Bob stood up and did a hand gesture to the members. Tell you what guys, let's just do our job, the best is yet to come! He said.

Most members left the boardroom, I could understand why they were not impressed but the store has to run and the winners team was to make it happen, it was time to start turning the wheels!

I guess this was it!

I was winding up my work and keeping my files into my folder's compartments

It was hard to believe Andre' was gone but everyone decides on what they want to do with their lives and Andre' made his decision to venture into something new and different, it must had been the best choice for him!

As the old saying goes, it's up to every individual person to decide on what Path to tread on or how to shape their lives. If it is success, go for it!

I thought to myself!

The only thing left was to work smart and make a difference just as members of this particular boardroom has changed lives!

The way managers think, approach and delegate duties.

How they have gone to different locations and became great leaders!

I looked around the room for a moment in thoughts...

There was nothing more to say...

I closed the boardroom door behind me and left...

The end.

About Me!

I Majored in Arts, studied abroad and became an Interior designer. I did not stop there because success means keeping an open mind to learning and expanding knowledge so I chose to enroll in other courses which included Business and development which led me to study Insurance, property Laws, regulations and health at The Insurance and Securities School Of America Scottsdale Arizona. Traveling around the world, just made my poetry writing better !

In 2006,I was awarded Poetry Ambassador status and named in WHO is Who book by International Poets Directory, Later same year I received medal of merit and E, MOFFET Award for outstanding Achievement in Poetry writing at a Poets convention held in Las Vegas Nevada. I conducted thorough research to bring this book to fruition. .This particular book is meant to inspire the reader and bring a clear but simple picture to anyone with dreams to a successful business the rest is for the reader to imagine the un- imaginable! Expected is a high level of success!. I still contribute part of my poetry writing to Society of Poets which in return also makes donations to Educational programs to support needy children. My Participation in charity is part of my mission to make a difference And make someone's life better!

As The Boardroom takes a break, Andre ponders.. what's next! Having learnt the tricks of the trade from Forster& Pete, the pioneers. He knows his team taking over can handle any giant! . New marketing strategies, hard work, sheer commitment is the key! Myles, new Guy has no choice, he must make it work, AL', Josh and Bob are a mile ahead! They never let personal Issues affect their performances, together they create the fire that never stops burning in their co-workers, they get the job done... By all means, there's no dead end, find your way around it! What a formidable force! Their competitors have yet to find out their secret to that amount of success.

www.ingramcontent.com/pod-product-compliance
Lightning Source LLC
Chambersburg PA
CBHW060626210326
41520CB00010B/1485